About This Book

Why is this topic imp

Because executive coaching has grown
human resource professionals and their
them know when and how to use coaching for their organizations. Most
of the books on the market are "how-to" books, with very little material
to assist HR people in becoming savvy consumers of coaching services. The
topics and materials in this book can serve as a practical guide to learn
more about what coaching is and how to best use it in the organization.

What can you achieve with this book?

In the authors' experience, HR professionals, clients, and others in organizations have many questions related to the practice of executive coaching. This book provides information on the process of coaching, when it is
appropriate to use it, and how the four key roles of HR professional, client,
boss, and coach can function together to maximize the effectiveness of
coaching. This volume seeks to equip HR professionals, their clients, and
others with the ability to make informed decisions about coaching for
themselves and for their organizations.

How is this book organized?

This book is divided into five sections. Section I provides a definition of
coaching, situations in which coaching is appropriate, and guidelines on
selecting a coach. The critical steps in the coaching process are explained.
Section II provides an understanding of the different roles and responsibilities of the HR professional, the client, the boss, and the coach and how
each of them interrelate to achieve a successful outcome for the coaching engagement. Section III highlights some special topic areas, such as
executive development, for which coaching can be utilized as a way to
accelerate the learning process. Section IV offers first-hand accounts from

clients on their experience of coaching. Section V provides reproducible resources and forms that can serve as practical, everyday tools to be used by HR professionals and others. The Appendix contains an executive breakaway section—material designed for the coaching client. The breakaway section, as well as the resources and forms, can also be found on the Pfeiffer website (www.pfeiffer.com).

About Pfeiffer

Pfeiffer serves the professional development and hands-on resource needs of training and human resource practitioners and gives them products to do their jobs better. We deliver proven ideas and solutions from experts in HR development and HR management, and we offer effective and customizable tools to improve workplace performance. From novice to seasoned professional, Pfeiffer is the source you can trust to make yourself and your organization more successful.

Essential Knowledge Pfeiffer produces insightful, practical, and comprehensive materials on topics that matter the most to training and HR professionals. Our Essential Knowledge resources translate the expertise of seasoned professionals into practical, how-to guidance on critical workplace issues and problems. These resources are supported by case studies, worksheets, and job aids and are frequently supplemented with CD-ROMs, websites, and other means of making the content easier to read, understand, and use.

Essential Tools Pfeiffer's Essential Tools resources save time and expense by offering proven, ready-to-use materials—including exercises, activities, games, instruments, and assessments—for use during a training or team-learning event. These resources are frequently offered in looseleaf or CD-ROM format to facilitate copying and customization of the material.

Pfeiffer also recognizes the remarkable power of new technologies in expanding the reach and effectiveness of training. While e-hype has often created whizbang solutions in search of a problem, we are dedicated to bringing convenience and enhancements to proven training solutions. All our e-tools comply with rigorous functionality standards. The most appropriate technology wrapped around essential content yields the perfect solution for today's on-the-go trainers and human resource professionals.

Essential resources for training and HR professionals

Executive Coaching: A Guide for the HR Professional

Anna Marie Valerio
and Robert J. Lee

Pfeiffer

A Wiley Imprint
www.pfeiffer.com

ISBN: 0-7879-7301-7

Library of Congress Cataloging-in-Publication Data
Valerio, Anna Marie
  Executive coaching: a guide for the HR professional / Anna Marie Valerio, Robert J. Lee.
    p. cm.
Includes bibliographical references and index.
  ISBN 0-7879-7301-7 (alk. paper)
  1. Executive coaching. I. Lee, Robert J., 1939- II. Title.
  HD30.4V35 2005
  658.4'07124—dc22   2004014812

Acquiring Editor: *Matthew Davis*
Director of Development: *Kathleen Dolan Davies*   Senior Production Editor: *Dawn Kilgore*
Developmental Editor: *Susan Rachmeler*   Manufacturing Supervisor: *Bill Matherly*
Editor: *Rebecca Taff*   Marketing Manager: *Jeanenne Ray:*

Printed in the United States of America

Printing 10 9 8 7 6 5 4 3 2 1

Contents

For my mother, Fernanda, and to the memory of my father,
Nicholas, whose love and encouragement taught me
valuable lessons about coaching and teamwork.
-AMV

For my children, my granddaughter, and my about-to-arrive
grandchild, who continue to teach me so much about
living and learning.
-RJL

Acknowledgments

We would like to thank our colleagues in the Society for Industrial and Organizational Psychology, particularly Elaine Pulakos and Bill Macey, who started this process and encouraged us to continue it.

Our sincere thanks go to the clients who provided their first-person perspectives on what it was like to be coached. Their stories have added a refreshing perspective to the volume.

We are grateful to our colleagues who read and commented on drafts of the manuscript: Deborah Butters, John Fulkerson, Martin Greller, and Amy Moquet.

For their assistance in researching several of the special topics, we extend our gratitude to Veronika Boesch, Marilyn Dabady, Michael Frisch, Marina Tyazhelkova, and Ann-Caroline van der Ham.

We are especially thankful to our editorial team, Matt Davis and Susan Rachmeler, for their professional expertise. Our gratitude also goes to the three anonymous reviewers whose insights and comments helped us to refine our ideas and the manuscript.

We would also like to acknowledge the warm support of Angela DiGioia, the late Ann DiGioia, and Marianne Lepre-Nolan. Their steady encouragement on this project was especially appreciated.

Introduction

. . . .

Getting the Most from This Resource

Purpose

The purpose of this book is to help human resource professionals and their clients become more savvy consumers of coaching services. With the wide array of coaching services now available in the marketplace, HR professionals need information to allow them to sort through options, ask discerning questions, and understand what constitutes successful coaching engagements.

Audience

This book is written for human resource professionals who need to know what coaching is and how it can be helpful. Some of you are responsible for bringing coaching services to your clients.

Another group that may find this book interesting is the prospective clients themselves, since they need to know what they're getting into and how to use coaching to best effect. We are aware that the term "client" is used by some people to refer to the employer generally, or to the HR professional, or even to the boss. In certain ways, of course, they are clients as well as the person who is the focus of the coaching. These people certainly receive value from a successful coaching assignment. For the sake of clarity, and because we believe he or she should be the *primary* client, we use that term to refer to *the individual who receives the coaching*. The "executive breakaway section" (found in the Appendix) contains information specifically tailored for prospective clients of coaching services.

The clients' bosses also have a key role to play in successful coaching. They constitute a third potential audience. Although most chapters are written directly to the human resource professionals, many are relevant to all three groups.

For HR professionals: This book will serve as your guide as you decide if and when to use coaching to help a client. The book contains very practical chapters on selecting a coach, setting up the relationship, supporting the process, and evaluating the outcome.

For prospective coaching clients: Our goal is to give you what you need to know in advance so that you can receive the greatest value from this investment of time and energy. Coaching can be a wonderful experience, offering life-long value, or it can be a marginal, mechanical ritual. The discussions and cases in the book will make you a knowledgeable consumer of coaching services. This knowledge will allow you to better manage your own expectations and to co-manage the coaching relationship in a proactive, productive way.

For the client's boss: As you know, helping your staff to solve performance problems and to develop their individual potential are central aspects of your responsibilities to them and to your employer. This book will help you with those tasks when you use professional coaches to help your employees. We identify the things only you can do to make coaching a successful experience for them.

How This Book Is Organized

The book has five sections and an Appendix:

- The first section explains what coaching is, who uses it, when and why, and when it should not be used. There is a brief discussion on the history of coaching, the varieties now in use, and the issue of selecting a coach. There is also a section on the coaching process itself, including a description of the typical steps in a coaching relationship.

- The second section clarifies the roles that each of the parties plays—client, HR professional, boss, and coach.

- The third section addresses selected topic areas relevant to coaching.

- The fourth section contains stories from clients about their own experiences of coaching.

- The fifth section has worksheets and forms that are reproducible.

- The Appendix contains an Executive Breakaway Section—material condensed from this book and designed specifically to help busy executives understand how they can be savvy consumers of coaching services.

Copies of the Executive Breakaway Section and all the forms and worksheets from this book can be found on the Pfeiffer website (www.pfeiffer.com).

How to Use This Book Most Effectively

Each chapter heading is framed as a frequently asked question. The discussions in each chapter are short, focused answers to those questions, with case study illustrations from our coaching practices.

The book need not be read sequentially. You may choose to go directly to particular topics on an as-needed basis. If you want an overall understanding of the issues associated with the use of coaching, then you may wish to read the book straight through. If you have a specific question about the use of coaching, you can go directly to the relevant chapter to obtain the information quickly.

We are aware that every organization uses coaching in its own way. We present what we believe are generally accepted best practices, although we know that dozens of variations occur for many good reasons. We hope that, whatever role you occupy, whether the HR professional, the client, or the boss, you will discuss with your colleagues any specific points where this book's suggestions diverge from your organization's practices.

Before moving on, we want to note three things this book does not try to do:

- We don't try to teach anyone how to do coaching. There are shelves full of books already on that topic. Some of them are listed in the bibliography.

- We don't address the use of coaching as a component of supervision. Some writers argue that bosses should manage by using coaching techniques. They make some good points, but that's not what we're talking about here. When we use the term "coach," we mean someone who does this for a living as a professional, although in some cases that person may be an internal employee of the company. Most of the coaches we're thinking about are external, either on their own, in small consulting firms, or in major consulting organizations.

- We do not attempt to explain how to set up an internal large-scale coaching program or to integrate coaching with an established leadership development program.

Section I

· ·

Coaching as a Service

This section of the book is designed to help you more fully understand what coaching is and how you can become a more savvy consumer of coaching services. The chapters in this section equip you with fundamental, practical knowledge: what constitutes coaching, when it is appropriate to use it, how to select a coach, and what to expect in a coaching contract. You will be able to gain a deeper understanding of how to go about incorporating coaching as another tool to help people improve their job performance. This section enables you to know what critical questions to ask of coaching professionals so that you can serve the needs of your organization.

Chapter 1. What Is Coaching? Here we provide a brief history of coaching and some of the rationale for its recent popularity in organizations as an effective learning methodology to stimulate executive development. Driving forces behind organizational change are listed. Definitions of different forms of professional helping are provided to draw clear distinctions between related terms.

Chapter 2. When Is It Appropriate to Use Coaching? In this chapter, we cover topics such as the types of situations in which coaching could provide the most value and the kinds of circumstances that lend themselves more to using coaching than using other forms of developmental learning methods. We explain what the coach and the coaching process contribute to the learning of "soft skills," such as interpersonal skills, communication, delegation, and adjusting to the fast pace of change. In this chapter you will begin to understand more about what actually happens in the coaching relationship and why coaching can be such an effective process. Conversely, it is also important to know when not to use a coach and when coaching will not have much of an impact.

Chapter 3. How Do You Select a Coach?   Here we provide some guidelines on finding a coach and things to look for in selecting the right coach. This chapter will help you to hire the professional who is most appropriate to the task. You will gain an understanding of the factors to think through when selecting a coach, such as training, experience, and skills and competencies. Since the chemistry between client and coach is so important to a successful outcome, this chapter provides some ideas on how to work with the client in selecting the coach. Finally, this chapter also provides some insight into things to avoid in a coach to enable you to prevent potential problems down the road.

Chapter 4. What Are the Steps in the Coaching Process?   In this chapter, we delineate the logical progression of the steps in the coaching process, such as contracting with the coach, setting goals, assessing results, action planning, and evaluation. In nearly all circumstances, a coaching process will begin with a general understanding among the client, the HR professional, the boss, and the coach about what is going to happen in the coaching engagement. You will learn about the importance of having a good structure for the coaching assignment and what elements should be in a good contract. Since one of the most important steps is having a clear understanding of the client's issues, what is to be accomplished by the coaching is a critical part of the initial goal setting. Brief descriptions of different forms of assessment data and their value, such as interviews, multi-rater feedback, surveys, and direct observations, shed light on how and why objective information can be very powerful. Various forms of action planning, or planning for development, are explained so that you can see what the client may need to do in order to learn new behaviors. If you know what questions to ask to evaluate whether the coaching process was successful or not, it can help you to determine whether the client remained on track and whether or not goals were achieved. This chapter poses some questions for you to consider to enable you to evaluate the overall outcome of the coaching process.

1

· ·

What Is Coaching?

This first chapter addresses the most elemental question of all: What is coaching? Many people have different definitions, so it's worth taking a closer look. Topics covered are

- A short history

- Driving forces behind organizational change

- Definitions of coaching

- Definitions of related terms

A Short History

Coaching is a term traditionally associated with athletics. Everyone in the sports field expects to receive a lot of coaching. There is no belief that good athletes come by their skills in some entirely "natural" way. That's why the people who run the teams are called "Coach" as their official title.

But that wasn't always the case. Perhaps you recall the movie *Chariots of Fire*, about a British Olympic team in the early 20th century. At that time the idea of hiring a professional coach to improve a track runner's performance was considered at least newsworthy if not scandalous. Today everyone in athletics uses a coach, and the coaches are expected to be competent professionals.

Coaching to improve organizational performance and to help bring out an executive's potential have also gone through a history of increased acceptance. There is no clear starting point for the use of coaching for executives, but according to some views coaching has been going on for fifty years or so under the labels of consulting or counseling. Most people agree, however, that it wasn't a common practice until the late 1980s or early 1990s; since that time it has generally been known as coaching.

In the earlier years coaching often was triggered when it became apparent that an executive was missing a specific skill, for example, not being able to speak effectively on television or to large groups, or in preparation for an overseas assignment. Often the reason to bring in a coach had to do with interpersonal issues, or possibly there were concerns of a "personal" nature having to do with health, career, or family matters. These situations typically had an aura of secrecy about them because of a desire not to let anyone know that a coach was being used.

Driving Forces Behind Organizational Change

Since the mid-1990s the world of work has changed drastically. The same forces that are changing our lives in organizations are driving the greater use of coaching (see Table 1.1). The demands placed on organizational leadership in the new business environment have expanded greatly.

Corporations have grown lean and have lost pools of talent in the downsizing efforts. Those left in charge often did not have the years of experience needed to inform their decision making. The pace of change in organizations had accelerated and a premium was put on speed. This meant there was precious little time for consensus building or intelligence gathering, and so the risk of errors by a leader or leadership team increased. Coaching emerged as the preferred "just in time" learning to help leverage the areas that would have the greatest impact on results.

Table 1.1   Driving Forces Behind Organizational Change and the
Use of Coaching

- Globalization of business, extending to vendors, resources, markets, and competition
- Flatter, leaner, more rapidly changing organizations, with the inevitable result that bosses have a harder time developing or even knowing their direct reports
- More teamwork and greater emphasis on lateral rather than vertical relationships
- Greater integration of the world economy and its attendant knowledge requirements
- Reliance on technology and a focus on e-business, plus the task of keeping up with the speed of obsolescence in the IT industry
- A fiercely competitive marketplace, with its premium on speed, savvy, and flexibility
- Increasing pressure to produce short-term financial results
- The need to optimize the talents of domestic and international multi-cultural workforces
- Expanded personal work demands placed on leaders related to global relationships and travel, business complexity, and faster organizational change
- The proliferation of alliances, acquisitions, partnerships, and joint ventures
- Shifts in values and priorities associated with younger generations, dual-career marriages, and both positive and not-so-positive changes in the larger worldwide society

As we write about coaching today, the aura of secrecy has been entirely dispelled. Coaching may still be triggered by a problem, but this is no longer viewed as "an issue." Executives are expected to be challenged with tasks they've never undertaken before or that may be entirely new to the organization. Additionally, many coaching assignments are initiated entirely to help the client grow as an executive, without there being any specific gap in skills or style identified before the coaching begins. Even when a problem has been encountered, an important goal of the coaching is to stimulate the client's overall growth and development, not just "fix" the problem.

It is not surprising, then, that greater numbers of larger and mid-sized companies and other organizations are using coaches these days. Coaches are not licensed by the government, and they aren't listed on a national roster. All kinds of people use the "coach" designation on their business cards. Coaches are also found throughout the economy, in entrepreneurial start-ups, family businesses, health care organizations, government agencies, and just about everywhere else. Coaching is well-established as a management practice throughout Europe and is growing as a service in Asia and Latin America.

Definitions of Coaching

A number of different definitions of coaching are available. For purposes of this book, we think of coaching as *a one-on-one development process formally contracted between a coach and a management-level client to help achieve goals related to professional development and/or business performance*. Coaching typically focuses on helping the client to become more self-aware through the use of action learning methods.

Some fine points about that definition should be given attention.

- "One-on-one" doesn't mean others aren't involved. The boss and HR manager are almost certainly involved. The client's peers and subordinates also may be. But this isn't team development, or mediation, or any other form of consulting that has a multiple-person client. Here it is clear that one person is the primary client.

- "Formally contracted" means this is very intentional and planned. There's nothing casual about a coaching relationship. It is a business deal and usually entails a letter or memo clarifying the terms of the deal.

- "Management-level" can mean anything from recently hired professionals up to the CEO. The client doesn't have to have a "manager" or "director" title, but should be a present or future participant in the leadership and managerial processes of the organization. This book isn't intended for situations focused primarily on craft, hourly wage, or administrative support employees.

- Some "goals" are related to short-term business results, while other legitimate coaching goals are focused on bringing out the future potential of the client. It's usually a mix of these issues. Goals that are too highly personal, however, are more properly addressed by a different kind of professional helper. Goals that are entirely business and not at all personal, such as changing a product's brand image, are outside the range on the other end.

- "Action learning." Coaching presses the client to do the learning. This happens by helping clients find and use good data about themselves and others and to develop a wider range of self-management and leadership skills. The coach doesn't show up with correct answers. The client does the hard work and is left with skills that should serve a lifetime.

One way to categorize coaching situations is along these lines:

- *Skill development*—typically an interpersonal or self-management skill

- *Performance*—problematic behaviors, new challenges

- *Development*—competencies needed for the future

The coaching we're talking about applies in all three of these kinds of situations. Sometimes the purposes overlap, and sometimes the goals extend in additional directions, but these are typical settings.

Definitions of Related Terms

Since terms can be overlapping and confusing. Let's take a look at some relevant distinctions.

Coaching vs. Consulting

When helping clients address goals related to business performance, the coach can sometimes function, in part, as a business consultant. Sometimes the distinction between coaching and consulting may appear to be blurred. That is because the topics of discussion in coaching sessions are framed within the context of organizational results that must be achieved. To help a client be successful, the coach must take into account both the client's strategic business challenges and his or her unique pattern of strengths and developmental needs. Successful coaching outcomes occur when clients develop the skills and abilities that enable them to attain specific goals. Consulting is more problem-focused and has a larger definition of the client—one consults to systems and/or organizations.

Other Types of Coaching, Mentoring, and Therapy

Life coaching is a form of professional helping that focuses entirely on the individual. Relevant issues include family, career, health, spirituality, finances, and community involvement, as well as performance at work. We would agree that a person who has his or her life in good order is likely to be a better contributor at work. However, the nature of the contract here is different (for example, wider scope, less tilted toward organizational outcomes), and the life coach needs a different set of skills.

Supervisory coaching occurs between the client and the boss, as was mentioned earlier. A boss cannot do what an independent coach does. The boss has much greater accountability for achieving results and for clarifying realistic expectations and standards. The boss has authority to take or recommend disciplinary actions, rewards, and other organizational actions. Sure, the boss can be supportive and helpful—but the boss is ultimately still boss. Coaching also calls for a high degree of confidentiality, which is not possible with bosses.

Mentoring has to do with long-term career sponsorship. A mentor normally is a highly placed executive who takes a stewardship interest in the performance and career of a younger professional. In a mentoring relationship, the focus is on career advising and advancement.

Therapy is provided as a mental health service by psychologists, psychiatrists, clinical social workers, and other therapists, that is, mental health professionals. It is appropriate when there is a painful and perhaps dangerous problem that needs to be corrected. Therapy typically has a greater historical focus than does coaching, which is present/future oriented.

Summary

To provide a starting point and some perspective, in this chapter we have covered a brief history of coaching and the rationale for its recent widespread popularity. Recent driving forces for organizational change have been highlighted and executive coaching has been defined and explained. To enable readers to understand the available options for coaching, mentoring, and therapy, the distinctions have been drawn among these different types of assistance and what they have to offer.

Looking ahead to the next chapter, we examine the kinds of circumstances under which coaching is most appropriate. You will begin to understand more about what really happens in the coaching relationship and about situations and settings where coaching may not be the best option.

2

. . . .

When Is It Appropriate
to Use Coaching?

What does a coaching opportunity look like? When is coaching the intelligent way to approach a situation? This chapter examines circumstances when calling in a coach makes good sense.

Topics covered in this chapter include the following:

- When coaching is appropriate

- How a coach can help

- When not to use a coach

Coaching situations don't exist in the abstract—they occur in connection with a particular person, at a particular junction in his or her organizational life. Therefore, what represents a business challenge and, hence, a coaching opportunity for one person may not be the same for another person. This seems obvious, but it's worth restating.

A fair percentage of coaching assignments start out because there has been a "glitch" of some kind—a complaint, a low rating on a 360° survey or a performance appraisal, unresolved conflict, or perhaps an unnecessary business problem.

Contributing to this glitch may be a personal trait or work habit, for example:

- A trait may now be creating performance limitations, even though it was responsible for success in the past.

- There may be a part of someone's style, perhaps considered a quirk or mannerism, that was tolerable before, but now is problematic.

- Something in the client's character may have been unnoticed at work until new levels of demand and difficulty brought it to the surface.

Our sense is that most coaching assignments begin when the client enters into a rapid learning phase on the job or is intentionally involved in a developmental program. Even many of the glitch situations often are reshaped into developmental opportunities.

There are lots of ways to learn. Our early educational lives were typically dominated by "instruction" in one form or another. As we grew into adulthood, trial and error became perhaps the most common learning method. We also learn by reading about what others have done, watching what others do, or occasionally by going to formal classes. Personal coaching is also a learning alternative, one that accelerates the learning process. Therefore, coaching is useful when someone has a need to learn to do things in new ways, wants to learn what is taught, and would like help. Generally, the things that need to be learned are related to what most of us call self-management issues, interpersonal skills, or the demands of leadership roles.

Something in the way of a business challenge probably is causing the need for this learning. This challenge may appear as a change in the nature or scope of work, an assignment to turn around or fix a business, or a global or international assignment with a high level of complexity and ambiguity in it. In the previous chapter we listed a number of important business trends, any of which can be causing this challenge to show up in your life. Usually these challenges occur in clusters, possibly creating feelings such as "It just never stops" or "I might be in over my head" or even "What am I supposed to do now?" Whatever it is, there is a need to ramp up quickly and accelerate the learning curve.

When Coaching Is Appropriate

Coaching tends to be most appropriate when:

- Performance makes an important difference to the employer. Almost by definition, the contributions expected of senior executives fall into this category. Managers at other levels who are in especially significant roles also are responsible for making an important contribution, so they too can be appropriate coaching clients. Managers may receive coaching simply because they are considered to be "high potential," regardless of the nature of their current organizational role.

- The relevant learning issues are in the "soft skills" area. Improving any person's performance in these areas is often difficult and requires an intensive effort. Many of these coaching assignments fall into familiar categories:
  - Helping people with personal or self-management issues, such as a need to micromanage, time management difficulties, or integrating work and family life.
  - Helping people who have assertive, dominant, or controlling styles become better able to build relationships, create trust, delegate, work in teams, or develop their subordinates.

- Helping people who have good "people" skills to be better at calling the tough decisions, setting and enforcing standards, and handling conflict in productive ways.

- Helping people develop leadership skills when they have moved (or are about to move) into a more prominent role. Some typical leadership issues are providing vision and strategy, performing symbolic roles, and functioning in a much more "alone" position without receiving much valid feedback.

- Used in conjunction with formal succession planning programs.

- Associated with executive development programs. With increasing frequency, lessons learned offsite may be combined with on-the-job assignments and the support of a coach when the formal program is over.

- People are struggling because there are no right answers. Clients need to develop their own solutions to certain of the puzzles of executive life and it's hard for them to do it on their own. If there were right answers hidden away somewhere, the task would be a lot easier.

- The learning needs to happen according to the client's schedule, and quickly. So timing is critical. People who are moved into important positions with little advance notice can be supported with a coach.

- Assimilating a new hire. Another term for this is "onboarding."

The common theme throughout this list is the need to deal with a steep learning curve. See "Common Coaching Situations" in Section V for a summary list of some common categories of coaching clients.

How a Coach Can Help

The previous discussion tells us something about what clients and their coaches are talking about. Interpersonal skills and styles, conflicting goals and values, keeping up with too many changes and demands, adjusting to difficult circumstances, finding good ways to get ahead in the company, discovering what "getting ahead" means these days, doing things more quickly—all of these can be part of coaching conversations. As we said earlier, coaching is usually about the "soft skills" that are in the spotlight when business challenges cause people to stretch into bigger or more complex assignments.

What actually happens in the coaching relationship that allows someone to become better at interpersonal skills, communicating, delegating, time management, emotional self-management, or other soft skills? How does someone focus on and improve these kinds of skills?

First, let's agree that these skills are not of the kind that can be learned in a classroom setting. Rather, they are learned by direct interaction with others while working. Sometimes this is called "action learning." This is the way adults learn best, and this is the model that best applies to interpersonal skills. With the coach's help, a feedback loop is created based on trying out new behaviors, followed by feedback and reflection, and then trying again to be as effective at whatever is happening.

In Chapter 4 we will go into some depth regarding the steps in the coaching process. At this point we'd just like to say something about what the coach and the coaching process contribute to the learning.

- *Focus of attention*. Having a coach means paying attention to the issues. Appointments are scheduled, time is spent, and discussions are held regarding the relevant topics.

- *Self-discipline*. Because of the regularity of appointments and the involvement of other people, it's a lot easier to stay on track. Organizational life is full of distractions, even emergencies. Having a coach is a way to increase the priority on this change effort.

- *Valid data*. Change and learning require good data, and the coach can help in that area. Information is needed on what the client brings to the job, what actions are being effective, and what is needed in order to succeed. A coach may offer his or her personal views of the client's actions and/or may do some "testing" using standardized inventories. The coach can interview others in the organization to obtain their views confidentially. The coach can help interpret 360° surveys, attitude surveys, or performance reviews. Perhaps most importantly, the coach can help the client make sense of all this data.

- *New ideas*. The coach may or may not have held a job similar to the client's. But he or she has talked to a lot of people facing the same issues and knows something about how those people have succeeded. The coach brings new perspective to the client's thinking and helps him or her to get out of mental ruts and dead ends. Not all the ideas are brilliant nor will they work perfectly. Nonetheless, there's a pool of suggestions waiting for the client to check out.

- *Support*. It's not easy to do things differently. In addition to their own ingrained habits, clients' colleagues may have them fixed in their minds as persons who do things in a certain way. Making changes means taking risks, persevering in the face of resistance, and possibly feeling a little strange or silly at times. Changes require a "safe" environment in which to take these risks. The coach is there to provide encouragement and help, and someone to talk to while all this is happening.

- *The learning process.* Sometimes the greatest value coming out of a coaching relationship isn't just changed behavior or the changed perceptions of others in the organization. Sometimes it is the client's insight into *how* to learn. The coach's expertise is exactly in this domain, and some of it should rub off over the course of the relationship.

A coaching assignment is triggered by an opportunity or a glitch or a transition of one kind or another. There will be many more opportunities, glitches, and transitions in life, but a coach won't be there for most of them. If the client takes away good insights into *how* to handle the learning/change process and a sense as to how to use these insights in future situations, then he or she is a real winner.

When Not to Use a Coach

Coaching, as with any other management option, can be attempted in situations that really call for something else. Before contacting a coach, one of your responsibilities as an HR professional is to screen the coaching assignments to determine whether coaching is the best option. The goal is to provide coaching when it is appropriate and only when it is appropriate. If the coaching process has already been started, it is possible that the coach might identify these issues. Although many situations are not clearly defined, here are descriptions of some settings where coaching is perhaps not the best option.

- If consensus has already built up that someone should leave the organization, coaching isn't likely to change that momentum. Coaching to give a person "one last chance" almost never works. Options to consider might be a transfer (if a large enough organization is involved) or a leave of absence. If these options aren't available, outplacement might be best.

- Sometimes a person is just in the wrong job. Selection and placement aren't exact sciences. Reassignment or reorganization may be called for, even if there are no hard feelings and everyone has been trying to make things work out well.

- Coaching cannot make much of a dent in situations in which success is due to factors beyond the client's control. Successful outcomes may be driven largely by technology, competition, regulatory constraints, or other factors. It's important that business problems not be blamed on one person before good business sense has been used to improve performance.

- Similarly, sometimes a poorly designed organization structure or management process can be the constraining factor. It pays to examine the systems within which the work is being done to see if they are designed as well as they should be.

- Some business situations aren't going smoothly for reasons that aren't as large as the macro forces (technology, competition, and so forth), nor as specific as the performance of one individual. It's possible that the small group, work unit, or team may need to be looked at as the client. These situations call for an organization development specialist.

- Significant personal problems can affect how things happen at work. We all know this, of course, but sometimes we forget it. Important emotional issues need to be dealt with by professionals trained to handle them—employee assistance programs, clinical psychologists, psychiatrists, social workers, and others.

- Career counselors aren't just for high school kids. People at all organizational levels, and at all ages, may be dealing with issues that are most properly helped by career counselors. Typical questions that arise for career counselors are "Am I doing what I should be doing?" "In what kind of organizations do I best fit?" "Am I the kind of person who should be taking on leadership roles?" "Is now the time for me to take that entrepreneurial plunge?"

- Just because many people are hiring coaches, it doesn't mean that everyone has to have one. Some organizations are regular users of coaches, to the point that everyone has to take a turn being coached. There should be a good reason to put in the effort required from both the client and the coach and a way to tell whether they have accomplished something.

- If the client just doesn't want a coach, then don't hire one. Sometimes it is important to have offered the coaching, and just having made the offer is important in itself. You may want to revisit the topic at a later time. There can be many reasons why a person whom you think should have coaching may decline. Perhaps he or she is afraid that coaching carries a negative overtone. Perhaps he or she thinks that it is someone else who needs the coaching. Maybe the client is simply wrong, but if the client doesn't want the coaching, not much good will happen. Being a client in a coaching relationship must be a voluntary decision. It can't be forced, and it shouldn't happen if it's "just for show."

Summary

In this chapter, we have examined when it is appropriate to use coaching and the circumstances that lend themselves more to coaching than to other learning methods. You have a better understanding of what occurs in a coaching relationship and when not to use a coach.

The next chapter will provide you with some guidelines on finding a coach and some things to look for when selecting a coach. It will help you hire the professional who is most appropriate to the task. Because many organizations employ both internal and external coaches, the benefits and challenges of each are discussed. Finally, you will gain some insight into some things to avoid in a coach to enable you to prevent some problems before they occur.

3

How Do You Select a Coach?

In this chapter we look at the practical issues involved in selecting a coach. The goal is to work with a coach who is appropriate to the task. That obvious statement, however, rests on the surface of a potentially rather complex decision.

In many companies the HR professionals will do most of the selecting. At the other extreme, the client may need to do all of the work to find a qualified coach.

Topics covered in this chapter include the following:

- Finding a coach

- Selecting the right coach

- Things to avoid in a coach

- Internal coaches

Finding a Coach

Before all else, be sure that what you need is an executive coach to help the client with issues of performance, potential, and leadership. Review the material in Chapter 1 so you know whether you should hire an executive coach, a life coach, a career counselor, a psychotherapist, or any of several other kinds of resources.

As with consultants or business service providers, coaches obtain much of their business through referrals. Asking your friends and colleagues for the names of good coaches is a good way to start. As a human resources professional, you are likely to have connections to local or national coaching organizations, and you can also make inquiries among your colleagues at other companies.

Selecting the Right Coach

Coaches should be recruited, screened, and interviewed in a manner similar to that used for other professionals. The client should also have a strong voice in having the final approval on a particular coach. Even if you as the HR professional do much of the screening, the client should participate actively in the choice as well.

As one HR professional in a health care management organization described coach selection: "We ask about the coach's capabilities. We find out what the leadership methodologies are in which the coach has been trained and if they are consistent with the direction in which we are trying to move the culture. Also, the fit between the person and the coach is important. There needs to be a connection so the client is open to listening and sees the coach as credible. It is very important for the coach to be non-judgmental. We seek input from the client on the comfort level with the coach."

In some organizations, the clients do the actual selection of coaches. You may or may not be that involved in the actual selection process. Your primary role may be as a conduit of information for the client. Whatever your role in coach selection might be, you can provide value to your client and your organization by raising some important questions that help to select the right coach (see "Questions for an Interview with a Prospective Coach" in Section V).

References

The question of references often comes up. Coaches are usually willing to provide references, but not all clients want to be used as references. It's easier to get references from HR departments than it is to get them from individual clients.

Size of Firms

Many coaches work as solo practitioners or have joined with a few others as a small firm. The resources to do coaching are minimal—there's no need for fancy offices or large overhead expenses.

There also are many coaches who work part-time or full-time for larger regional or national consulting firms.

Some very good coaching is offered by people who were or still are in the mental health field, such as clinical psychologists and social workers. Coaching is sometimes offered by large employee assistance firms. Career counselors and life coaches sometimes also do executive coaching. For the past ten years or so, especially under the constraints of managed care, a number of such professionals have been retraining themselves to be coaches to clients in organizational settings.

Chemistry

None of the factors listed in this section will have any importance if there is not good chemistry between the client and the coach. No one has a formula for defining good chemistry, but "you know it when it's there" nonetheless.

Perhaps good chemistry, in this case, is some combination of trust, respect, likability, and overall comfort. If the positive connection is there, the coaching is more likely to succeed, regardless of anything else. One doesn't need an elaborate explanation to explain a strong gut reaction—intuition can be trusted.

A note of caution, however. Some people carry a notion in their minds as to what a coach should look like. The coaches you meet may not look like that stereotype, but may be exactly right. Try to keep an open mind as you interview prospective coaches so you won't pass up a good coach in favor of one who fits a stereotype.

Education

There really aren't any schools offering academic degrees in coaching. Still, a large number of coaches have degrees in "the helping professions," such as psychology, organization behavior, counseling, and so on. Some clients are more comfortable working with these coaches because they know that underneath almost all business problems there lie personal issues as well.

Psychologists, in particular, have expertise that makes them extremely well-suited to provide coaching services. This book is authored by two psychologists, and we are speaking from our perspective. However, we do believe that psychologists have a strong foundation from which to practice. Psychologists have training in assessment and diagnostic methods at both individual and organizational levels. They understand how learning and decision-making processes occur. Schooled in measurement of behavior change, psychologists can provide help with devising metrics for leadership development interventions. Also, the professional activities of psychologists are guided by a code of ethical conduct.

Some clients strongly prefer a coach with extensive business experience and don't care as much about the behavioral science aspects of the coach's education. There are a wide variety of "coaching skills" programs available to people who want to practice coaching as a profession. These programs are offered by consulting firms and in some cases by universities via non-degree programs. They range from two days to a year in length, and, of course, they vary widely in terms of focus and quality.

Certification

Certifications are provided by organizations offering training programs. This service has evolved in recent years as the coaching profession has taken shape. Minimally, it is an indication that the coach is serious about this work and has invested a degree of effort and time into obtaining the designation of Certified Coach. Most coaches do not have this certification, however, including a large number of very good ones.

Another kind of certification has to do with the use of certain proprietary tests or surveys. The publishers or owners of these materials permit coaches to use them after certain requirements have been met, such as attending short training programs on how to use them properly. You may wish to ask whether a coach uses these measuring systems and is certified to do so.

Experience

Coaching has been around long enough now that you can expect your coach to have relevant experience at this work. How much? What kind? These are tough questions, and there are no correct answers.

The amount of experience to expect will increase when selecting a coach for more senior-level clients and/or for those who have a more complex set of issues to work on. It is not unreasonable to expect that a senior-level coach will have ten to fifteen years of business experience and at least five years of coaching experience. If a client is in a middle-level role and has straightforward issues to deal with, the coach need not be as experienced (or as expensive!). In all cases, the coach should have enough organizational experience in general to appreciate the realities the client is living with and be able to bring good "political" insights to the relationship.

When asked about how coach selection decisions are made, one HR professional from a large technology company stated: "We need coaches who have had expertise in coaching and organizational development. I generally look for someone who has coaching experience with individuals at the same level as the potential client and who has had experience in the same industry. It is very important for the coach to have credibility in the eyes of the client and to be familiar with complex organization issues. The coach needs to help the client navigate through many challenging situations and, as an

HR professional, it is important to feel confident in the decision to use a particular coach."

There is some benefit to you if the coach has already done work in your organization or at least in your industry. However, it's probably not wise to overly limit yourself in that way, especially if you are in a small organization or in a specialized part of the economy. Coaches have learned how to work in new environments. It is appropriate to ask about the coach's experience in this regard and to ask about his or her willingness to learn what needs to be known to do the work well.

If you have a very specific problem, it may be worthwhile searching around for a coach who knows about that topic. Examples of specific problems might be

- Expatriate adjustment

- Diversity or sexual harassment concerns

- Leading virtual teams

- Ethical dilemmas

Skills and Competencies

Following is a list of competencies to consider when selecting a coach. It is loosely based on a Corporate Leadership Council (2003) report addressed to corporate buyers of coaching services.

Getting Started

- Able to establish an intimate and trusting relationship with the client; bonds well with the client; creates a sense of optimism and safety

- Establishes a useful coaching contract

Structuring the Relationship

- Designs and creates appropriate action plans and action behaviors

- Develops plans; establishes and revises goals with the client

- Manages the client's progress and holds him/her responsible for action

Interpersonal Effectiveness

- Is fully present, conscious, and spontaneous—demonstrates authenticity

- Actively listens—really hears what the client is dealing with

- Asks powerful questions

  - Has good insights into the informal and political issues within organizations generally and the client's organization in particular
  - Has good insights into human issues—understands interpersonal relationships
- Communicates clearly and directly

- Creates and raises the client's awareness; serves as an astute observer of the client's behavior and is good at providing constructive feedback

Self-Management

- Practices in an ethical manner; treats people and information with dignity and discretion

- Appreciates the issues that are important to the wide diversity of clients in the organization

Working with the Client in Selecting the Coach

A reasonable way to involve the client in coach selection would be to have an early discussion with the client in which you come to agreement on the following topics:

- What criteria to use for coach selection. Using some of the criteria outlined above, you and the client can determine which factors are important and how a particular coach meets the desired criteria.

- How to proceed in meeting and screening coaches. After you have found one or more potential coaches, it is likely that you as the HR professional will conduct the initial interview. You will need to determine at what point the client enters into the process and weighs in with an opinion.

- How the final decision will be made. This may work differently depending on the level of the client in the organization and the culture of the organization. After consideration and discussion of all relevant criteria, both you and the client must have confidence in the coach you have selected and expect that the investment of time and resources will have a successful outcome.

Things to Avoid in a Coach

Coaches aren't perfect, of course. There are some danger signs, however, that are good predictors of potential problems. They tend to fall into two categories—how the coach works and who the coach is.

Some coaches have settled on "the one right way" to do coaching, and neither wish to nor can use alternatives. This kind of inflexibility opens up possibilities for disputes about how, when, or what needs to be done. Rigidity of style is a matter of degree, of course. Sometimes the coach really needs to take a firm position on a topic. But if it happens too often, the problem may be more with the coach than the client.

Another working issue is an overloaded schedule. Coaches cannot schedule their new clients—business comes in whenever it happens to come in. Coaches cannot schedule when their clients have crises or go on long vacations or business trips. Each client thinks—and perhaps deserves to think—that he or she is the only client the coach has, but that's obviously not the case. How many clients should a coach have at any one time? There's no magic number, but there shouldn't be so many that the coach can't find time for each client when needed.

In terms of who the coach is, two related points are worth mentioning. The first has to do with big egos. The goal of coaching is to make a success out of the client, not the coach. Everyone wants to look good, but a coach can't do that at the expense of a client. On the contrary, the coach must be the client's cheerleader. Why would a coach want to display a big ego? Because coaches sometimes do self-serving things, or perhaps that's just the way the coach is wired. Whatever the reason, it's not good.

A related issue has to do with authenticity. Being a coach isn't just a role, and the coach shouldn't be wearing a mask that says, "I'm a coach." Coaching requires truly human connections, not role playing. The coach needs to connect to the client, to hear and feel what the client is thinking and feeling, and to respond with genuineness.

Internal Coaches

In some large organizations, there are professionals who do coaching of other employees. These internal coaches do essentially the same job as their external counterparts. It may be a full-time job, or they may have other duties as well, such as leadership training, succession planning, or organization development.

Internal coaches, embedded in an organization, are usually connected with HR in some capacity and usually provide other services as well as coaching. Sometimes they may be doing internal coaching exclusively, even if it is on a part-time basis. The department within HR sponsoring internal coaching usually also contracts for and manages external coaches. That way, both types of professional coaching can be coordinated and complement each other. In fact, often the head of such activities spends some of his or her time as an internal coach.

Internal coaching is just now emerging as a valuable HR offering and will continue to "professionalize" as time goes on. It is similar to more traditional external coaching in some ways, but has important differences. It provides important value to employers and clients, and is a positive additional service, along with external coaching, in full-service human resource environments.

Benefits

As organizations seek greater efficiency, accountability and cost effectiveness, there are some obvious benefits associated with an internal coaching capability. The per-assignment cost can be lower, when there is a large enough number of assignments to justify the start-up costs. An obvious advantage is that an internal coach brings considerable knowledge of the company and may have access to a great deal of "real-time" information about the client. Also, there can be greater flexibility in scheduling. Finally, continuity may be more possible over a period of months or years. Although internal coaching is not likely to totally replace external coaching, an appropriate mix of the two approaches seems to work well in many settings.

Tradeoffs

Some tradeoffs exist regarding the use of internal coaches. Organizational level is one of them in that sometimes the more senior-level clients want to receive their help from outside coaches. Confidentiality has to be considered differently when the coach is internal. Particularly complex or sensitive assignments will call for a coach with specialized experience that may not be available internally.

Clearly, the internal coach should not be in the same chain of supervision as the client. The coach cannot be an agent of the boss. Still, there is a heavier obligation on the part of an internal coach to draw clear boundaries around what is to be shared and what is not. Internal coaches often have a burden of proving they are adequately independent. Certain clients may really prefer to have an external coach for this reason; most clients don't seem to care one way or the other.

Another issue relates to credibility. Credibility comes with time and reputation, of course. Initial credibility can be artificially higher for outside consultants—not just for coaches, but for all kinds of consultants. The internal coach may need to pay some attention to positioning within the organization. For example, the coach may have to be "sponsored" by a top executive. On the other hand, the internal coach may need to avoid being tabbed as having the office where troubled employees hang out.

Only recently, and still in limited ways, training programs for internal coaches have appeared, mostly as an outgrowth of external coach training. At this point, however, there is little professional literature specifically targeted to internal coaches, and no professional meetings or "special interest groups" within larger associations. Internal coaches, who often have other HR duties as well, may spend virtually all of their time "on the inside" and may not have the time to acquire professional support for the coaching work that they do. This must be guarded against.

Guidelines for Addressing Key Challenges

Some guidelines can be offered to meet some of the key challenges for internal coaching. First, internal coach selection should be formalized. In some very large companies, there have been efforts to create rigorous selection processes to evaluate candidates against required competencies. At the very least, it will be beneficial to think carefully about these issues. Selection by "default" or done casually will be both ineffective and highly risky.

Second, there should be ongoing development for internal coaches. While some or all of such development could be waived based on professional training and experience, internal coaches—even more than external ones—must have a common philosophy and approach, as well as a forum to consider organizational challenges and opportunities. Companies should carefully think how to achieve commonality where it is needed without unduly constraining the flexibility of the coach. Organizations might well utilize the knowledge and expertise of psychologists who do executive coaching by enlisting them in the training and support of internal coaches.

Third, beyond the "who" of internal coaching is the "what." Before an organization offers internal coaching, goals for the service should be defined. Where it is housed is often linked with goals (that is, human resource planning versus training and development), so that must be considered too. Aligned with goals, coaching programs themselves must be described and standardized. For example, organizations have carved out assimilation/new leader, development planning, and skill-focused coaching programs to be delivered by internal coaches. Tying together all of the three points above, a set of assessment tools and concepts should be selected, their use taught, and their application woven into the programs offered.

Fourth, internal coaches are more likely to be challenged by confidentiality issues. Internal coaches may have multiple roles in the organization. This could be confusing to clients. Organizations must decide in advance how those challenges will be handled and provide opportunities to discuss especially complex or pressured situations. Some of the answers to confidentiality issues reside in how internal coaching programs involve the client's boss and how those programs are "advertised" internally. In addition, an internal master coach or peer coach support group may be important in sorting through challenges to confidentiality. Dealing with this issue has to be somewhat "over-engineered" for internal coaching to take hold and grow.

A final topic of possible interest here has to do with having multiple clients in the same organization. This is always true for internal coaches, but can also be true for external coaches who have been working around the company for a while. There are benefits as well as challenges associated with this issue. "Discretion" is the important point. Each client deserves to be treated as an individual, without having to worry about intentional or accidental disclosures. In theory, there should not have to be a problem here, and there seldom is.

External and Internal Coaching Can Co-Exist

External coaching and internal coaching should be viewed as complementing each other, rather than competing with each other. An organization may benefit from using a combination of external coaches and internal coaches. As a knowledgeable HR professional, you can benefit from having a pool of coaches from which you can draw when client requests come in. For example, external coaches may be more appropriate for clients who are more senior and at high levels in the organization. Some clients who are resistant to change or tend to be very defensive may be more open to working with someone from outside the organization. In these situations, issues of coach credibility and confidentiality will be critical. As one HR professional in a health care maintenance organization stated: "Using an external coach promotes a great way of learning. The advantage of using an external coach is that the client does not have to be concerned about letting down his or her guard, as he or she would be with an internal coach. There is no suspicion of an ulterior motive with an external coach, so it is easier for the client to focus on the learning. For the HR professional, there is no need to worry as much about crossing boundaries and a fear of sharing secrets with others in the organization."

Alternatively, if you have several high-potential clients who are still at relatively early career stages, then internal coaches may be advantageous to use. The internal coaches are more likely to have access to performance appraisals, multi-rater feedback surveys, and direct observations of the clients. They can build these observations back into the coaching.

In short, there will be some clients for whom internal coaches are very appropriate, and others for whom external coaches will be a better match. You may want to be able to provide the organization with the flexibility to serve all client situations as they arise.

Summary

In this chapter, you have been given some guidelines for finding and selecting a coach. You have gained an understanding of the relative importance of the coach's training, education, experience, and skills. The benefits and challenges for both internal and external coaches have been discussed. You have also had the chance to increase your insight on some things to avoid in a coach.

The next chapter delineates the logical progression of the steps in the coaching process: contracting with the coach, setting goals, assessment, implementation and action planning, and evaluation. You will learn about the importance of having a good structure for the coaching assignment and the elements of a good contract. The value of different forms of assessment data and of using multi-rater feedback in coaching will be discussed. Common elements that may occur during implementation and action planning are described. The rationale for the evaluation of coaching and some sources of data that may be used in evaluation are provided. Finally, the greater use of electronic coaching is considered as a future trend.

4

What Are the Steps in the Coaching Process?

Coaching relationships are custom-designed, not replicated from a manual the coach keeps on a shelf or that the HR department asks external coaches to obey. However, a large percentage of coaching assignments do follow a general format, which is what we will outline in this chapter. If you feel your situation falls outside of the usual pattern for coaching assignments, you will need to contract for a variation on the traditional relationship so you develop a process that makes sense for you and your company. In this chapter we will also address the way coaches and clients can use technology to aid in their relationship.

The Coaching Process

Steps in the coaching process usually are delineated at the outset of a coaching engagement. Although the names and labels may vary, in almost all situations a coaching process will contain these steps:

1. Contracting
2. Initial goal setting
3. Assessment
4. Implementation and action planning
5. Evaluation

1. Contracting

Coaching is possible only when there is mutual agreement. Regardless of whether there is a formal, written contract, there has to be an initial step in which a general understanding is reached with the HR professional, the client, the boss, and the coach about what's going to happen. You may wish to set up an initial meeting with all parties to discuss the issues. See "Agenda Items for an Initial Discussion" in Section V for some pertinent questions to be covered at an initial meeting.

Usually the agreement is more formal with the HR professional and the organization and less formal with the client. A continuum of formality is possible, ranging from a one-paragraph email to a formal contract with a non-disclosure agreement. Sometimes the agreement is shared with the client. A sample agreement for coaching services can be found in Section V.

The purpose here is not to create rigidity or arbitrary limitations. Rather, a clearly understood coaching process is important because predictability builds trust. A good structure also allows for discussion of variations to the plan, as needed.

Perhaps the most important element in the success of a coaching engagement is the bond or "chemistry" between client and coach. A lot has been written, but very little decided, on what goes into the magic of a good bond. During the contracting step, there has to be a sense from both parties that "this is going to work" or "I trust this person." Of course, the relationship can be terminated at any time later on, but there must be positive feelings at the outset—or there is no contract!

Beyond good chemistry, what else is in a good contract? Often there is a memo or letter of agreement addressing these points:

- How often the coach and client will meet and for approximately how long, for example, two or three times each month for about an hour

- A starting and possible ending date

- The general focus of the coaching, such as project leadership skills, an abrasive interpersonal style, time management, or work/family balance issues

- Some sense of how "success" will be measured—how the wrapup and evaluation might proceed

- Reporting and confidentiality—who can say what to whom

- Costs (if the letter is going to the person who pays the bills)

When asked about which steps are most valuable to the coaching process, one HR professional from a large technology company replied: "The contracting phase is critical to do with the client and the client's supervisor so that there are appropriate expectations set by everyone involved. All of the parties involved—the client, the boss, the HR person, and the coach—need to understand the goals and objectives of the coaching. It also helps to convey to the coach the possible future plans for the client and what is contained in a succession plan if one actually does exist for that individual. At that point, it is incumbent on the coach to develop a coaching plan to help the client achieve the desired goals."

Confidentiality

One of the main requirements in coaching is trust. Any successful coaching relationship is built on mutual trust between the coach and the client. The relationship is based on privileged communication between client and coach, and often the information that is exchanged may be potentially damaging. If there is a breakdown in trust, the coaching engagement is clearly bound to fail. Therefore, the issue of confidentiality is crucial to coaching.

Information Sharing.   When being coached, the client will share delicate private and corporate information with his or her coach in order to explore developmental opportunities. Naturally, this situation may cause concerns from the client's perspective as well as from the coach's perspective. A client might wonder who else has access to the information. How can he or she be assured that the information is not shared with someone he or she doesn't trust? Who knows that he or she is being coached? Will the information shared have an impact on promotion or salary?

The coach, who is usually paid by the client's organization, faces a different conflict: Am I obliged to share a progress report with my client's supervisor, Human Resources, or the sponsor? If so, how much do I go into detail? Who in the organization has to be informed if my client shares information about illegal wrongdoings involving either the client or other organizational members? All these concerns are legitimate and must be addressed in the contracting stage before attempting to build a trusting, open relationship.

If the client believes that the coach is sharing private information or if the coach feels caught up in an organizational power struggle, the relationship is likely to crumble. Confidentiality is therefore both an ethical and a practical issue.

Ethical Standards.   Whereas doctors, lawyers, and priests, whose professions require dealing with personal information, are bound by the law to apply certain ethical standards, there are no explicit laws in that regard applicable for coaches. For those coaches who are psychologists, the ethical standards concerning disclosures in the profession of psychology apply. Although the coach has to try to make every effort to honor the client's confidence, the coach can not provide a guarantee. Clients need to be informed that their information is not privileged under law.

Best Practice.   In order to avoid conflicts, the coach is well advised to discuss the issue of confidentiality up-front with the client. By making the client aware that there are usually other stakeholders in the coaching process, such as the supervisor, the HR manager, or others, the coach can discuss with the client which information is shared and which information is kept confidential. Ideally, during the contracting phase, a meeting of the coach, the client, the boss, and the HR professional has occurred in which issues of confidentiality have been discussed. Who does the reporting? How much write-up is needed? It makes sense to share information about goals and progress, but not the contents of coach-client discussions.

The other possibility is to encourage the client to inform other stakeholders about his or her developmental process. This can either be done in the presence of the coach or in private. In any case, the coach and the client must reach a joint agreement that leaves them both in their comfort zones and sets a solid basis for a trusting relationship. By reaching an agreement about confidentiality in the first place, most conflicts of interest can be avoided.

2. Initial Goal Setting

A first draft of goals—What is to be accomplished by the coaching?—should be part of the contracting step. It may look like a simple thing to do, but it is not.

- Client, coach, HR professional, and boss all may wish to see somewhat different outcomes. These expectations have to be articulated and conflicts explored and resolved.

- As the coaching process evolves, what is considered to be a realistic and desired goal may change.

- There may be interim goals as well as long-term goals.

- There may be "business" and also "personal" goals, and they may overlap and impact each other.

A reasonable approach, therefore, is to set an initial goal and expect to confirm or revise it as time goes by.

Goal setting is central to the process. Well-defined goals allow you to work together, to assess progress and success, to choose appropriate methods and relevant data, and so forth. Good coaching is results-oriented and doesn't wander off into unimportant tangents. It is important for the coach to understand the business challenges facing both the client and the organization.

The goal for many coaching engagements is expressed in behavioral terms. For example, the client will do more or less of something, or learn to do something, or stop doing something. Some typical goals in executive coaching address client improvement in leadership competencies, specific interpersonal and social competencies, and the ability to manage his/her career issues. Other goals may explicitly and implicitly involve increasing the effectiveness of the organization and team.

When possible, it will be useful to define the coaching goal in "business" terms—connecting it to operating plans or financial measures. This is often not possible, however desirable it might be. It is generally sufficient for the goal to be agreed on by the four interested parties—client, coach, HR, and boss. Both the client's needs and the employer's interests must be served. This agreement may be easy to reach or may be negotiated.

3. Assessment

Good coaching rests on a foundation of good data. It is important for the coach to quickly ascertain the performance level of the client in order to understand the magnitude of the gap between current performance and future desired performance. How is the client currently functioning? What has to improve or change for the client to maximize performance? The coach has to determine the overall pattern of strengths and challenge areas to help the client set goals for improvements in job performance. The coach and the client must be able to operate together with a common language and set of concepts. The most efficient way for the coach to go about this is by systematically collecting data on those behavioral dimensions that have the most impact on performance. Why collect data? Executives like data. The issues should be described in "non-arguable" terms. Multiple perspectives create a richer picture. Coaching shouldn't be based on hunches, and objective data is of value. The data have to be consolidated, integrated, and prioritized.

Data gathering can be done in lots of ways. Some alternatives for gathering information are described below:

- *Interviews*. The coach will create an interview protocol and conduct either individual face-to-face or telephone interviews. Interviews can be conducted with direct reports, peers, supervisors, and others in the organization who have a high degree of familiarity with the client. The results from the interviews are summarized separately and reviewed with the client, along with the data from other sources.

- *Multi-rater feedback assessments*. Sometimes these are also called "360-degree feedback instruments." In addition to making "self" ratings, usually the client is asked to provide a list of raters from the following categories: direct reports, peers, current and past supervisors, and customers. Most multi-rater feedback tools are now available so that the entire administration is done electronically. Typically, once the client has provided the raters' email addresses to the survey administrator, the raters receive a web address and a password. When the raters access the website and type in a pre-assigned password, they can take the surveys at their convenience. Reports may be generated electronically and emailed to the coach, who delivers the feedback to the client.

- *Testing.* Some coaches use individual psychometric tests. Some tests require professional qualifications, either through a certification process by the publisher or by educational background. In the hands of a competent practitioner, they can be very helpful. These include personality tests, interest inventories, learning styles, and interpersonal style tests.

- *Existing qualitative and quantitative data from performance appraisals, attitude surveys, customer satisfaction surveys, and training programs.* The information from these sources can be very helpful to the coach, particularly at the start of a coaching program, because it provides insight into how the client is being perceived by various parts of the organization.

- *Observations of the client.* Experienced coaches have skills in observing and recording behavior, and the information gathered from direct observations of the client during meetings, phone calls, and presentations can be very useful. The coach may also ask to see written materials from the client such as emails. All of this can provide powerful real-world data, especially when combined with data from assessments.

How much historical data to include? This depends on the nature of the client's issues. It can be really helpful for the coach to understand client behaviors that may have a long history. And it can be helpful for the client to reflect back and gain greater self-awareness and insight. However, the focus of the coaching needs to be on how the behavior will become more adaptive in the present and future.

Using Multi-Rater Feedback in Coaching

Larger organizations often develop their own multi-rater forms, which reflect the behaviors or cultural issues of importance to the organization. Consulting firms and publishing companies offer dozens of forms for specific applications—supervision, sales management, leadership, and so on. If properly chosen or developed, a 360-degree feedback rating form will address important, relevant dimensions and will be a good foundation for coaching.

Multi-rater feedback can be used to support coaching, either to help a client develop his or her potential or to address a performance concern. Such data can be useful for identifying developmental needs of future leaders. It is helpful for communicating behaviors consistent with new organizational values or principles or to provide senior leaders with valid data so they can make fine-tuned adjustments to their leadership styles. Typically, results are shared only with a client, who now "owns" the data.

The 360-degree feedback methodology is used because it provides the coach and the client with a language and a set of concepts with which to conduct their sessions. Multi-rater feedback can be used together with personality tests, appraisals, or other data sources. Depending on the style and model used by the coach, multi-rater feedback can be used as a source of information to validate concerns the client has, to better define issues that are not well understood, or to explore for possible "soft spots" that might cause trouble in the future.

In some situations, there may already be existing multi-rater feedback, and the client can allow the coach to gain access to it. The data may have been part of a leadership development program, or it may have been generated for administrative purposes. If it is recent and appropriate, the data will serve its intended purposes as an impetus for self-reflection and action planning.

In many organizations 360-degree data collection is regularly used for "administrative" purposes, such as performance evaluation or making decisions about promotions, compensation, or perhaps even retention. One component of this application will be a formal feedback session in which someone goes over the data with the employee and may use it to begin a coaching process. In this situation, the person doing the feedback—usually the boss or an

HR professional—has to address the shift in purpose of the data and also a shift in role from "evaluator" to "coach."

Coaching can be a critical step if the organization wants to get the most value from the feedback process. It is the job of the coach to help the employee confront the information provided by the raters. Together the coach and the client can work on converting the feedback into an action plan useful as a framework for personal development. Coaching can be a single event or it can be extended over a period of time. The goal is to make the client accountable for using the feedback as a guide for performance improvement. Coaching puts 360-degree feedback in context, makes it pertinent to what has to be achieved, and generates creative, practical development plans.

What Should an HR Person Know About Multi-Rater Feedback?

Here are several important points that should make using 360-degree feedback a success, especially in combination with coaching:

- Don't force it on a client. Sometimes, of course, these assessments are used company-wide for all managers. When that is not the case, then the use should be voluntary.

- It may be best to ask the client to identify most or maybe even all of the raters. Most people will be reasonable about who they choose. It is important that the client not "stack the deck" by including only raters who have a highly favorable opinion of the client! Using a broad variety of raters results in more credible data.

- Not everyone knows what is involved in a 360-degree feedback process. If there is any doubt, take the time to explain to the client and to the rater what it is, what it does, how it is used, and its benefits to all concerned.

- Provide information on the purpose and process to assessors when giving out the questionnaires.

- If the data is to be kept confidential, make that point clearly. If others will have access to it, those people should be identified.

- Even if a professional coach facilitates the feedback, it is important for the client's manager and HR representative to be familiar with the rating instrument and how it is used.

Advantages of Multi-Rater Feedback

- Feedback based on 360-degree data tends to be more balanced than the single opinion of a manager, no matter how objective the manager tries to be.

- A systematic 360-degree report will bring out viewpoints that might not otherwise be heard.

- Because it is so broadly based, it is almost impossible to dismiss negative elements.

Some Cautions About Multi-Rater Feedback

- Responses to the rating scales may be somewhat different when peers or direct reports believe the results will have career or compensation implications for someone, as opposed to knowing that the data will be used only for developmental purposes. There may be a tendency toward more favorable responses when it is used for appraisal or compensation purposes.

- If the multi-rater instrument was custom-developed by your organization, your coach may need to acquire some familiarity with it. Don't assume that your coach will immediately understand all of the language used in

the instrument. You may need to provide some expla-
nations for the dimensions of behavior that are rated so
that the coach can understand why they were chosen
to be measured and how they fit in the organizational
culture.

- This method of data collection does take time from
  many people—at least six or seven respondents, and
  sometimes as many as twelve or more. If there are a
  number of coaching clients in the same organization,
  they may be using an overlapping set of raters. At times
  there may be a bit of groaning about the additional
  workload.

Need for Reflection Following Feedback

Once the data have been integrated and summarized, the coach will
feed back the information to the client, usually over more than one
session. Because there is usually much information to reflect on, it
is better if the client absorbs only some at a time. Sometimes the
client is surprised by certain aspects of the data and needs time to
reflect and think it all through.

After the data from assessments and other sources has been
reviewed, it makes sense to go back to the goals that were created
earlier to see if any new ones should be added and to reprioritize
those that have been retained.

4. Implementation and Action Planning

The coaching process can move into an implementation and
action-planning phase when:

- The initial goal of the coaching has been determined

- The coaching agreement has set expectations for how
  the coaching engagement will proceed

- The coach has had the opportunity to become familiar with different aspects of the client's behavior from the assessment results

In helping a client explore and learn new concepts and skills, coaches may employ a variety of coaching methods and techniques. Which methods a coach may choose will depend on the background and training of the coach, the unique interaction between the client and the coach, and the coach's views on which approaches would be most effective within a given organization. Fundamentally, a coaching process allows a client to take the time to reflect on and explore issues that affect the client's and the organization's effectiveness. Although every interaction between a coach and a client is unique, some of the common elements that could occur during implementation are:

- *Exploring for alternatives.* The client benefits from gaining greater self-knowledge by understanding his or her feedback data, reviewing previously successful and unsuccessful efforts at behavioral change, gathering new ideas, reading, and observing others. In their sessions, the coach frequently poses questions to encourage the client to engage in reflective thought. The coach provides a supportive relationship in which the client is stimulated to explore new ideas, feelings, and behaviors. Often, the role of the coach is described as that of a catalyst.

- *Experimenting with new behaviors.* The trust that is established between the client and the coach enables the client to experiment with new behaviors that may feel very foreign initially, but that, in the long run, add to the client's repertoire of adaptable responses. Some of the techniques that help clients to feel more comfortable and competent as they adopt new ways of interacting with others include

- *Rehearsing or role playing.* Being able to practice possible responses to anticipated situations lets clients polish skills and reduce some of the anxiety associated with the fear of the unknown.

- *Visioning.* Professional athletes have known for quite a while that increments in performance can be realized just by imagining oneself giving a peak performance. Whether it is a competency, such as speaking to a large audience or maintaining one's composure during meetings, if clients can practice visioning optimal performance, they are partway there.

- *Problem solving.* Coaches generally are good at asking clients questions to stimulate their thinking to arrive at creative solutions. The idea is that eventually the clients may learn to do creative problem solving on their own.

- *Role clarification.* Understanding everyone's role in a given business/social situation can help clients to act appropriately and pick up important social cues. Coaches can help clients foster role clarity for themselves and in their organizations.

- *Creating an action plan.* An action plan consists of several components. It can be used to establish a goal, define the measures that will be used to determine whether or not the goal has been reached, and to explain the actions to be taken to reach the goal, the resources needed, significant milestones, and completion dates. This type of action plan can be used by the coach and the client in tracking development goals. In Section V, you'll find a sample action plan as well as a blank form that you can reproduce for your own use.

- *Gathering support and feedback from colleagues.* The chances of a successful coaching outcome are enhanced when the client can be open with colleagues about the desired changes. Enlisting their commitment increases the likelihood that the client will receive accurate feedback as new behaviors are explored and practiced.

- *Devising a long-term development plan.* This may be optional for the client and focuses on personal goals over a longer time frame. Sometimes the client can use it for career management and to advance profession-ally. A long-term development plan can serve as prepa-ration for future roles and contributions. It can also help the client avoid backsliding once the coaching assignment is over.

5. Evaluation

There are many good reasons to evaluate the results of a coaching assignment. First, you will want to know whether the client's performance is improving. Has this individual succeeded in making the behavioral changes needed to improve leadership? To stay informed about progress on goals, you may want to receive occasional reports from the coach. A sample progress report is provided in Section V.

Second, you will want to determine the impact of the coaching on others in the organization. Has the allocation of resources yielded results for both the client and the organization? How do others perceive the changes that are occurring?

Third, the evaluation serves as a recalibration process. It can provide valuable information for the coach and the client that helps them make adjustments in the coaching. Which new behaviors are being demonstrated and which ones are not? How does the focus of the coaching need to shift? What job experiences does the client need at this juncture? What feedback should the boss provide to the client at this point in time?

Fourth, the outcome of the evaluation can serve as powerful reinforcement for the work effort involved in coaching. What successes can the client and coach celebrate? Where are renewed efforts required? What should be the content of the boss's communications to the client in order to provide both reinforcement and incentive?

Finally, the evaluation can show where the action plans require updating and revision. Are the coaching goals still appropriate or do they need rethinking?

A good time to specify the details of an evaluation of the coaching program is at the contracting phase. An evaluation process can help in establishing clarity at the outset about what the coaching is designed to accomplish. The memo or letter of agreement can address the topic of how success will be measured.

When it comes to a formal evaluation, a number of approaches are possible. The methods used for gathering information during the assessment phase can be used as measurements of performance between the initial data collection (Time 1) and a later point (Time 2). It's a good idea to allow at least six months between Time 1 and Time 2 to allow the client the opportunity to develop new behaviors. It also takes time for others in the organization to notice the client's new behavior patterns! One or two demonstrations may not be convincing evidence for others to accept that a client is truly doing things differently.

Evaluations can be based on any of the following sources of data:

- *Interviews*. If interviews were done at the start of the coaching engagement, it may be appropriate for the coach to reassess or reinterview the same respondents and compare responses from Time 1 to Time 2. How do the interview themes between Time 1 and Time 2 differ? Is the client demonstrating more adaptive behaviors and fewer disruptive ones?

- *Multi-rater feedback assessments*. With this form of feedback, it is especially important to wait at least six months before a reevaluation and to recognize that it is the pattern of changes that will be significant.

- *Informal feedback from others*. On a more informal basis, the boss and selected individuals may be asked how the client is doing. This information can be written in a progress report that is completed by the coach or jointly by the coach and client. With the exception of the input provided by the boss, it is a good idea for the feedback to be aggregated so that statements cannot be attributed to one person alone. Protecting the anonymity of raters ensures that the feedback will be more accurate and reduces raters' fear of reprisal.

- *Performance appraisals, attitude surveys, customer satisfaction surveys, and training program surveys*. Since many of these measures are administered infrequently, they may or may not coincide with the evaluation period of the coaching program. Also, the actual questions on surveys often change from year to year so that the measure from Time 1 to Time 2 may not be consistent. With the possible exception of the performance appraisal, these instruments may not be sensitive enough to pick up the kinds of behaviors that the client is attempting to change. However, taking all of this into account, the coach may still want to see the results from these sources of data, especially if at least a year has elapsed from the time of both the first measurement and the start of the coaching program.

- *Client feedback*. Is the client satisfied? Feedback from the client may be given directly to the coach, or to you, the boss, and others in the organization. If periodic progress reports are written jointly by the client and the coach, the client may have the opportunity to provide more formal feedback. Often, however, the client will simply tell you how valuable the coaching has been in accelerating the required new learning. You may even notice a change in the client's "self-talk" or "reframing" of situations. Is the client more realistically aware? Did the client learn something important?

- *Action plans*. The coaching may have involved the creation of an action plan that defines goals, measures of success, and completion dates. Was the action plan created and implemented successfully? Were useful goals set? Were the goals achieved? Is there a business outcome? A behavior change? How did the organization benefit from the action plans?

- *Long-term development plans*. Sometimes coaching leads to a long-term personal development plan. Was this prepared, and is there agreement to do something about it?

Finally, a good contracting process will provide some sense of how the coaching program will be wrapped up. You will want to stay informed about that final phase of the coaching process. Did the client and coach openly discuss what has and has not been achieved?

Sometimes, there is a clear ending after a relatively intense process. More frequently, the coaching is continued with less-frequent sessions or on an as-needed basis and becomes an informal relationship with some level of paid involvement. There may also be a "planned follow-up" after a specified period of time. Usually, some closure is needed on the more formal, intense phase of the coaching. However the assignment ends, you will want to have evaluated the overall outcome for both the client and the organization.

Coaching Electronically

In the future, coaches are likely to do more coaching via the telephone and the Internet. There are several reasons for this trend:

- *Globalization*. Organizational functions will continue to become more global in nature. Clients' coaching sessions may not be able to be scheduled when both coach and client are in the same geographical location.

- *Cost-effectiveness*. It can be more cost-effective for coaches to deliver services electronically.

- *Technological improvements*. The improvements in voice quality in cell phones, computers with video, and other technological devices have increased the level of comfort in conducting long-distance conversations about personal/career issues.

Use of Emails

Many coaches will use emails as a way of following up on points made during a session or will send information on topics related to the client's goals for the client's use between sessions. Emails can be very effective in fostering clients' abilities for reflection. They require that senders be more thoughtful in their choice of words, and they allow readers more time to review and think carefully about the contents.

Whether or not emails are utilized more in the coaching process, the steps in the coaching process should remain the same. Usually, the initial contracting and goal setting can still occur via several face-to-face meetings in which the coach and client have the opportunity to forge the chemistry essential to a good coaching relationship. The ability of the coach to see facial expressions and body language is important for the coach to get to know the client. It also allows the coach to create a visual picture of the client, to more accurately interpret the client's communications, and to see exactly what others also see when they engage with the client.

Assessments

The electronic administration, scoring, and feedback of tests and assessments has made data-gathering more efficient and rapid. Because feedback from assessments still requires some careful interpretation, however, many coaches will provide an overall summary from the various data reports. The summary can then be delivered either electronically to the client, in face-to-face sessions, or in some combination of both.

Cautions

Over time, the coaching with an individual client might shift from face-to-face sessions to a greater preponderance of electronic coaching. In those circumstances, the coach must pay extra attention to the value of the message content. In making the comparisons between face-to-face and electronic coaching, the coach has to monitor the quality of the interactions. Are topics covered in the same depth? Is the client using the same richness of language? Does the client express feelings as readily? The coach should solicit feedback to find out whether the client is comfortable with the quality of the interactions via email.

Summary

In this chapter you have been shown a logical progression of the steps in the coaching process: contracting, goal setting, assessing results, action planning, and evaluation. You have learned about the importance of having a good structure for the coaching assignment and what elements should be in a good contract. You have been given brief descriptions of different forms of assessment data and their value, such as interviews, multi-rater feedback, surveys, and direct observations. Various forms of action planning for development were explained so that you can see what the client may need to do in order to learn new behaviors. Finally, this chapter posed some questions for you to consider to enable you to evaluate the overall outcome of the coaching process.

The next section describes the roles played by the HR professional, the client, the boss, and the coach. You will learn how each role, and the teamwork needed across the roles, contributes to a successful coaching outcome for both the client and for the organization.

Section II

• •

The Roles Involved in Coaching

This section clarifies the roles that each of the parties plays—the HR professional, the client, the boss, and the coach. For the coaching process to be successful, all parties must be able to fulfill the expectations of their roles and work as a team.

Chapter 5. What Is the Role of the HR Professional?   In this chapter we clarify the significant role of HR professionals as "stewards" for coaching in their organizations. HR professionals often can position coaching as an important HR strategy that helps executives achieve business results. We review the tasks for management of the overall coaching process and the support of all of the phases of coaching assignments.

Chapter 6. What Is the Client's Role?   This chapter enables the HR professional to learn more about the client's role so that he or she can be more instrumental in helping clients understand more about their roles. This chapter also provides some insight on what the client might be experiencing during the coaching process.

Chapter 7. What Is the Boss's Role?   This chapter enables the HR professional to learn more about the boss's role in the coaching process. This role may include identification of the need for coaching, rewarding progress, and providing the budget for the coach. The HR professional can help the boss understand his or her pivotal role in providing feedback and support to the client in the coaching process.

Chapter 8. What Is the Coach's Role?   This chapter enables the HR professional to understand the activities that are the coach's responsibility. These activities include structuring the coaching process, communicating with others in the organization, and setting the boundaries for the coaching relationship.

5

What Is the Role of the HR Professional?

The role of the human resources professional certainly is a very important one in the coaching process. In most organizations, coaching budgets or approvals lie within the domain of Human Resources. This can be one of the more gratifying roles you perform. It can also be frustrating because it deals with so many intangible issues and mostly occurs out of sight.

The HR person is a multiple-direction bridge between the boss, the client, the people who serve as information sources, and the external coach. The metaphor of a "bridge" is helpful in that it emphasizes that connections are made and traffic (information) flows in all directions. You need to understand the needs of all of these stakeholders. You are often called on to assist in smoothing the way for the relationships to work well. You may be depended on to be the knowledgeable advisor regarding how coaching will be deployed in the organization so it will dovetail with current or future development programs.

As one HR professional from a high-tech firm explained: "The communication between the coach and the HR professional is critical to the success of the coaching effort. The HR professional brings an understanding of the business that is critical for the external coach. The coach needs the information from the HR professional in order to understand the company's culture. So it is very important that they work well together for the coaching to be effective. I have also found that good communication is so important between the HR professional and the client's boss so that the HR person can provide the coach with further insight on the supervisor's observations. At very high levels in the organization, the client's supervisor may meet more frequently with the HR professional than with the coach. That means that the HR person may be in the habit of obtaining more up-to-date feedback from the boss. Passing along this information to the coach improves the coaching outcome because the coach is able to adjust the coaching content to suit the client's and the organization's needs."

The image of a bridge can, however, be somewhat misleading in that it is passive. If you are the responsible professional in an organization with an established coaching program, you may have to actively manage both the overall coaching program and, to some extent, each of the assignments. If you are not in an organization with an established program, you will need to manage each of the individual coaching engagements. In this chapter we will touch on many of the tasks HR people usually handle in regard to their coaching–oversight responsibilities.

After reviewing these tasks, you may come to the conclusion that "managing" just isn't the right word to use here. True, there is no good way to manage all these activities in the same way as one manages events that are largely under your own control. Coaching doesn't easily yield to standardized performance expectations and timelines. Different assignments use different measures of success. Almost all the really important things happen when no one else is watching or listening. Confidentiality blocks full communication.

Nonetheless, it is a reasonably manageable process. It takes time and effort to build all the appropriate relationships, of course, and to develop a "feel" for when things are going well. For the HR manager who is new to coaching, it may feel like a really slippery responsibility. But before too long you should bring coaching activities comfortably under your purview—even if it never becomes easily measured and managed. Used properly, coaching can be a powerful addition to your ability to accomplish things in the organization!

For the sake of discussion, we've separated this chapter into three parts:

- Manage the overall coaching program

- Support the start of new coaching assignments

- Support the coaching during and at the end

Manage the Overall Coaching Program

The organization and your immediate managers expect you to manage the coaching resources. There are several "to-do's" to keep in mind as you fulfill your role as the "steward" for coaching in your organization:

1. Clarify your strategy. If your job requires that you manage an established coaching program, you may first have to find out how the strategy for the program was set. If you do not have an established program, the questions you may want to ask include: What is the purpose of the coaching? How does it link to the business strategy? Is coaching done for remediation or for the leadership development of high potentials? What are the circumstances under which a coach will be considered?

2. Connect coaching to other development efforts. If your organization has a program for executive or management education, you may want to determine how coaching may be used to reinforce the lessons learned from the more formal classroom setting. How does the coaching reinforce lessons learned in training? How can the coaching be used to enhance on-the-job experiences?

3. Develop a pool of coaches. Where does an HR person go to find good coaches? There is no national registry. Through experience and networking with HR colleagues, a list can be built. It is then up to you to create the process to select the right coach for the needs of your organization. What are the skills and abilities needed in a coach for your organization? For this client?

   As one HR professional from a high-tech company puts it: "HR professionals need to make sure that they have someone who is capable as a coach, who has the interpersonal skills and recognizes the balance between the individual and the organization. You can't use the same coach for all people. You need a few different coaches in your back pocket."

4. Be an effective gatekeeper. Develop criteria for determining when coaching is needed. Coaching should not be used in situations where it is very unlikely to succeed. Non-successes will happen anyway, but situations that are loaded against the coach are just a waste of time, money, and reputations. What are the criteria to determine whether coaching is needed or not? Requests for coaching may come from anywhere in the organization. Your first task is to see whether it's really a coaching situation (you may wish to refer to the material on "When Coaching Is Appropriate" in Chapter 2). Sometimes saying "no" will be tough on your relationships with others, but it has to be done. There also will be times when you should be the one to initiate a discussion about bringing in a coach with either the client or with the client's boss. Sometimes the gatekeeper needs to open a door that others didn't even think was available.

5. Monitor the PR. In the course of your other activities, keep alert to what's being said about coaching. Is it seen as a valued, positive alternative? We all know that some coaching assignments begin because there's a "problem" or an "issue"

causing concern. Other assignments are entirely focused on helping bring out the potential in talented people. We also know that coaching can be more successful in some cases than in others. Your task is to know what the buzz is regarding this service and, if possible, do something to move it in the right direction. What can you do to help the organization realize the value of coaching as a methodology?

6. Support the executive as being the client. Coaching involves multiple stakeholders, including yourself, each having a claim to the title of "client." You can provide a service to everyone if you can make it clear that the individual executive is the *primary* client. We believe that coaching flows most naturally and most effectively when the individual executive is viewed as the client. We recognize, however, that other legitimate stakeholders are the organization, the boss, and you, the HR professional. How can you help the other stakeholders understand that the executive is the primary client?

7. Provide an orientation to the organization for the coach. In order for a coach to help the client set appropriate goals, it is important that the coach understand the structure of the organization and the strategic plans that guide the client's performance. If the coach can have the benefit of obtaining information from an insider's perspective, there is a greater likelihood that the coaching will be effective because the coach will have a context for assigning importance to some behaviors and not others. At a very basic level, the coach is better equipped to guide the client toward behaviors that will be in greater alignment with the organization's goals and strategies. How can you help the coach understand the organization's strategic business plans and the role that the client plays in those plans? What are the key informal relationships about which the coach needs to know in order for the coaching to be effective?

Beyond organization charts and strategy statements lie the informal, subtle things that impact the client's success. Some people call this "culture." It has to do with "how we do things around here." The coach needs to know—and eventually will learn—about dress codes, levels of formality, how influence is exercised, how decisions are made, and how people "win" in this organization.

In the words of one HR professional working for a large, Fortune 500 company: "Once the coaching engagement has begun, the HR professional cannot just walk away from the client issues. The client is not operating as a silo, but rather is operating as part of a system. That means that the organization needs to work on its systemic issues at the same time. The HR professional needs to be sure that the coach understands the climate and culture as they exist now as well as what the organization intends them to be in the future, so that the coaching can occur within the right context."

Every consultant knows that every client organization has some kind of "soap opera" going on just below the surface. There are alliances and antagonisms, perhaps resulting from events long ago or from more recent acquisitions or reorganizations. There are friendships and possibly even family connections that aren't evident to a newcomer. There may be romantic attachments, current or former. There will be winners and losers in the struggles for advancement. The coach doesn't need the entire story, but should be apprised of the elements that most directly impact the client.

8. Be realistic about information and expectations. There may be several reasons why little information is forthcoming from either the coach or the client. Since initial interactions between the coach and the client involve the establishment of trust, both parties will want to maintain confidentiality. Also, the process itself may unfold over time and it may be

easier for one or both parties to describe the interactions and milestones reached only in "broad brush strokes." Finally, if a contract has been established that defines the development plan, then periodic confirmations that the plan is on track may be all that client and coach will communicate to the HR professional.

See the "'To-Do' List for Managing Coaching Resources" in Section V for some questions to ask yourself as you fulfill your stewardship role.

Support the Start of New Coaching Assignments

When a client has been identified as a potential candidate for a coaching intervention, you will want to consider the following set of tasks that are important to the start of a new coaching engagement.

1. Make sure this is really a coaching assignment, not a problem that should be fixed some other way. Make sure the client is appropriate for this kind of investment and wants a coach.

   Most organizations have well-defined methods and procedures for dealing with personnel issues. As the HR person, you are, no doubt, very familiar with most, if not all, of them, and may even have authored some for your organization. To maintain the integrity of the coaching process, it is important to verify in advance that the appropriate intervention is, in fact, coaching, and not some other process or procedure such as performance management, employee assistance, or informal coaching from the supervisor.

2. Help identify the "right" coach, which often comes down to an intuitive choice once an initial screening has happened.

Helping your clients select the "right" coach will have enormous benefits for your clients, your organization, and your reputation as a valuable professional. You have a golden opportunity to demonstrate your knowledge and understanding of the best questions to ask in coach selection (see Chapter 3). Having to choose among options allows the client to rely a bit on "chemistry" or "intuition," which will enhance decision making and make it more likely that there will be a good match between the coach and the client.

3. Arrange for clear contractual relationships—not always a written contract, but there has to be at least some discussion.

It is always wise to set up a written contract that specifies the terms of the coaching engagement. However, even with a written contract in place, there is no substitute for the personal interactions and discussions that can occur between you and the coach. There are many good reasons for you to become better acquainted with the coach to assist you in the kinds of decisions you will need to make regarding the coaching assignment.

If, for some reason, a written contract does not exist, then having an understanding of the expectations and knowledge base of the coach becomes even more important. It is important to hold periodic conversations with the coach regarding the progress of the client, next steps in the process, organizational expectations for the client, and anything else that might impact the coaching assignment.

4. Help connect the coaching to important business objectives. For the coaching to be truly effective, both for the individual and for the organization, the rationale for the coaching has to be linked to business objectives. What are the business results that the client must achieve? What are the skills, abilities, and behaviors that the client must demonstrate in order to achieve these business results?

5. Share all the relevant data, including the client's future potential, with the coach. Relevant data can include many different things such as information pertaining to the client's past history and future potential in the organization, observations of the client's behavior from yourself and others, and data from corporate opinion surveys. In short, anything that may provide insight to the coach concerning the client's character, current situation in the organization, or career trajectory will be important for you to share with the coach.

   In your HR role you may be privy to succession planning information related to the possible next steps in the client's career. If the client is viewed as having high potential, then there may be some plans already in place for the next several assignments. If the client must successfully navigate the coaching intervention for career progression to occur, then this fact should be communicated to the coach as well.

6. Discuss with the coach how the assignment will be managed—what has to be shared, with whom, when. You will maximize the effectiveness of the coaching process if communications to relevant members within the organization are planned and coordinated with the phases of the contracting process. Your role in the management and communication of the coaching assignment is very important. How the coaching is perceived by the organization is critical to the success of the effort. Together with the coach, you will want to give some thought to the language that is used, the timing of the communications, and the appropriateness of the persons with whom the information is shared. You will want to be proactive in your role and check in with the coach periodically to see how things are progressing.

7. Help the client gain access to other sources of information, as appropriate. In your role as the bridge between the client and the rest of the organization, you may be in a position to have

some knowledge about both the relevant leadership issues with which the client is dealing and, simultaneously, about the topmost organization development concerns. Quite often, these two apparently separate issues are linked. You are in a position to assist the client in advancing his or her coaching goals by helping the client to gain access to sources of information that could enhance or accelerate his or her ability to learn and adapt to the ever-changing organizational environment.

Support the Coaching During and at the End

Because your help is needed to ensure that the coaching assignment stays on track, that the client commitment remains strong, and that the coach stays connected to relevant organizational issues, you will want to consider the following set of tasks:

1. Be open to discussing shifts in the goals for the coaching. Initial issues may not be the useful or complete definition of the scope of the assignment. Very often the client issues are initially defined in terms of behaviors that have been observed by others and obtained from a consensus of opinion. This "presenting problem" may only be the "tip of the iceberg," and it is incumbent upon the coach to diagnose the true issues. The coach, together with the client, may determine which behaviors should be modified in order to have the greatest impact. As the coaching process evolves, goals may shift for many reasons as the client gains practice in behavior change and as the salient issues in the organizational environment also evolve. Your flexibility and openness to discussion with the coach and the client concerning the future scope of the assignment will add value to its outcome.

2. Make sure the coach and client are staying on track and are in contact with any other people who need to be involved. Periodic contact with the coach and the client is important for obtaining feedback on whether the coaching engagement

is proceeding as planned. Since you are the primary point of contact, you may need to determine who else should be involved and make those suggestions to the coach and the client.

3. Help the coach and client evaluate and wrap up the assignment. Goal attainment, behavior change, new skills, better ability to make decisions or deal with complexity, more accurate self-perceptions, improved functioning, more data collection, client satisfaction, business results, reactions of other people to the client's new behavior. . . . How do you know whether the client is making progress or not? What kind of feedback must you seek out to determine whether or not the coaching objectives are in the process of being reached? If the goals have been set up appropriately at the outset of a coaching engagement, then steps in the achievement of some of those goals may be reached relatively early. It is reasonable to expect that there should be evidence of some behavior changes within the first two months of the onset of the coaching, even though different skills are acquired at different rates.

More complex skills will take longer to develop than simpler skills. For example, improvements in presentation skills may be evident sooner than changes in organizing and planning capabilities. Rates of learning may vary depending on the individual, the complexity of the new skills being acquired, opportunities to practice those skills, and the resources and support of the organization.

To evaluate progress and to help you determine whether or not the client is moving toward the attainment of stated goals, here are some questions you may want to ask:

- What are the changes in behavior and skills thus far? Does it appear as though progress is being made?

- Does the client have more accurate self-perceptions and improved functioning in the areas needed?

- Is the client better able to make decisions?

- How satisfied is the client with the coaching experience?

- What business results are to be expected if behaviors improve?

- What are the reactions of interested stakeholders such as the boss, direct reports, and peers?

Summary

In this chapter, we have clarified the significant role played by HR professionals as "stewards" for coaching in their organizations. You have learned more about the three aspects of the HR professional role as they relate to coaching: managing the overall coaching program, supporting the start of new coaching assignments, and supporting the coaching during and at the end of the assignment. To help you manage your coaching resources, you have been given some critical questions to ask yourself as you fulfill your stewardship role. You have been advised of some the ways that you can support the start of new coaching assignments. Finally, you have learned about some of the most effective tasks that you may assume in order to maintain your support during and at the end of the coaching assignment. To help you evaluate progress toward goals, you have been given some questions to ask regarding the client's behavior and its effects on the organization.

In the next chapter, you will learn more about the client's role to help you understand more about what the client may be experiencing and how you can be instrumental in the client's success.

6

. . . .

What Is the Client's Role?

You, the HR professional, play a pivotal role in the coaching story. We assume you would like to learn more about the client's role and what the client might be experiencing during the coaching process. You can be instrumental in helping the client understand more about his or her role, so in this chapter we examine the client's role in helping to ensure the success of the coaching relationship.

Coaching puts the client in a very *active* role. Nothing much of importance will happen as a result of coaching unless the client wants it to happen. All the other participants in the story are supporting characters. It is really all about the client and what the client wants to do.

This active role starts at the very beginning, when the first discussion is held about coaching. The client should have made an active decision to be a coaching client. Perhaps you, the HR professional, or perhaps the boss initiated the idea. Similarly, you may have been actively involved with the choice of who the coach would be and on what improvement areas the coaching will focus. However, ideally the client should enter this relationship with positive energy and curiosity.

The client should be comfortable about doing the coaching at this time. By "this time" we mean that the flow of the client's work suggests that coaching might be helpful now, and the client is comfortable with both you and the boss as participants.

So now it's time to actually start the coaching relationship. What should you be doing to help make it worthwhile for the client? What is the client likely to be experiencing during the coaching?

Topics covered in this chapter are

- Normal anxieties

- Ground rules and trust

- Taking responsibility

- The business relationship

- Time commitments

- Responsibilities to the boss and to the HR person

- Coachable moments

Normal Anxieties

At the very onset of a coaching engagement, it is "normal" for the client to feel anxious and vulnerable. The client is starting on a high-disclosure, high-vulnerability adventure with a stranger! There's only so much comfort one can gain from an initial chemistry-check meeting. The contracting sessions should help start the coaching process by reaching mutual agreement about goals and confidentiality, the methods to be used, frequency of sessions, and so on. Still, the client may feel a lingering sense of uncertainty as he or she embarks on an unknown journey. For the coaching to have a successful outcome, resulting in change and personal growth, it is wise to recognize that these feelings may accompany the client at the outset.

What might the client be anxious about? One answer to this question is that *all* changes come with some amount of stress. This is true for weddings, benchmark birthdays, promotions and new jobs, the birth of children, relocations—all the transitions and milestones of living, even the most joyous of them. Unhappy events certainly bring out a number of unsettling emotions, also. Coaching is associated with some degree of change in the client's public leadership style, and that too can be a transition. The outcome may be only a fine-tuning or a minor adjustment, but it may lead to something more substantial as well. Either way, the client may feel as though the world is watching and that there is more pressure from the increased scrutiny.

Another source of anxiety has to do with what happens if the coaching turns out *not* to be successful. The client may wonder: Was it my fault? Does it mean that a dead end in my career has been reached? Is my career derailed or plateaued? Has my fatal flaw been discovered? In almost all cases, these are just anxieties and not likely to be realities. Coaching isn't a surefire solution to problems, nor is it guaranteed to make the most of an opportunity. Many executives use a number of coaches over the course of their careers. We discuss the issue of measuring success elsewhere in this book. What's important to state here is that it's not uncommon for a client to worry about these things. These anxieties can be discussed with the coach, of course, or with the boss, or with you, the HR representative. Our experience suggests that these concerns quickly fade away in most cases.

A comment is useful here regarding human "flaws." A much better word might be limitations, sore spots, things we're not proud of, even our secrets. Coaching does go better when there is a free exchange about motivations and personal histories. However, it is perfectly within the rights of the client to draw limits. For example, the client might mention a messy divorce, a troubled childhood, a severe medical problem, or a traumatic military experience. There's no obvious need to go further than that. If that history isn't relevant to his or her current or future position in the organization, then it may be best either to omit it from the current coaching process or deal with it elsewhere.

Sometimes people are anxious about letting go of habits or styles they've owned for many years. The client might be feeling something like "I wouldn't be me if I didn't do things that way" or "I really don't want to stop being an analytic, detailed kind of person." Coaches are aware that some aspects of our characters are very deeply ingrained. Coaching isn't about deep character reconstructions. It's more likely to be about managing how this character shows up at work.

Ground Rules and Trust

One of a coach's first tasks is to create "safety" in the relationship. This topic is discussed at length in books about coaching and in training programs for new coaches. It is his or her job to make that happen, but the client has a role to play as well.

The structure of the coaching engagement serves as a roadmap for the client's interactions with the coach. By following the steps in the coaching process, as described in Chapter 4 or as agreed on by the coach and the client, there is a framework with a beginning, a middle, and an end. The framework allows the client to set expectations appropriately, recognize milestones and time limits, and celebrate successes. A planned journey along a well-lit path allows for more trust and cooperation. Discussions between the client and the coach about the ground rules will take much of the mystery out of the journey and will help the client to understand how to make the relationship work well.

Initially, the client may have many concerns about the coaching engagement. Encourage the client to ease whatever concerns he or she might have by asking the coach the questions that are on his or her mind. There is no such thing as a dumb, honest question. All first-timers have questions, whatever it is they are doing. Often some of the early inquiries "get the ball rolling" and lead right into important areas for further discussion. By asking the questions without letting them simmer, the client will feel more comfortable and build trust with the coach. Trust between people is built slowly over a series of many interactions, so the early experiences with the coach are critical for establishing a strong relationship. The client must feel reassured that the coach "has what it takes" to serve as a guide through the journey of self-exploration and personal development.

Coaching engagements evolve over time. There's no way to know exactly how things will progress, or whether revisions will be needed in the ground rules, the goals, or the methods. Encourage the client to feel free to talk about these with the coach.

Taking Responsibility

The client should be the "owner" of the goals for the coaching and for the steps for achieving them. When these are reasonably clear to the client, then the best course for the client is to move forward boldly. The client must accept feedback from whatever sources—assessment instruments, official appraisals, informal comments, the coach's interviews—and make good use of it. The client will have to engage in some behaviors that may make him or her feel uncomfortable, such as trying new ways of doing things, getting feedback from people who saw the client do things differently, learning what helps and what doesn't. The coach can serve as a catalyst, but ultimately it is only the client who can make change happen. You can help the client by acknowledging where the responsibility lies and that it is normal to feel some apprehension.

Coaching requires that the client give voice to his or her thoughts, hopes, and feelings. If this is not something the client normally does, then at first it may feel as it does when one is exercising an unused muscle. The client needs to work through this and keep going. It will come more easily when the client accepts the ownership and responsibility for making a success of the coaching effort. The coach can only be a catalyst—the client has to make it happen.

This is obvious, but not easy. Why is it difficult? For the same kinds of reasons that diets, good health habits, and New Year's resolutions are difficult. Just because it makes sense doesn't mean we'll do things that way. We're accustomed to putting blame on other people, procrastinating, expecting others to change first, even being lazy. Recall the corny old joke that goes "How many people does it take to change a light bulb? Only one, but the bulb really has to want to change." It's really not so funny when we think about all the good intentions we've had that went nowhere, and not for good reasons at all.

So what can the client do to overcome this tendency? A few hints: Go public with the planned changes—it makes it harder to backslide. Enlist the support of others; ask for their active support. Keep a log or diary of efforts and successes. Reward themselves when things go according to plan.

The Business Relationship

The relationship between client and coach is a business relationship: the client and/or the client's organization purchases professional services from the coach to help both the client and the sponsoring organization. There are likely to be both short- and long-term business benefits.

The outcome of the coaching benefits many others beyond the individual who receives the coaching, including direct reports, peers, supervisors, and anyone else who may be affected by a strengthening of leadership in one part of the organization. A ripple effect of good things can be created when the changes in behavior of one individual are perceived by others in the organization. This is especially true if it is the leadership of a boss or a peer that is strengthened. Improvements in the morale of a group can occur. Individuals may be inspired to start on their own agenda for personal growth. The "return on investment" from successful coaching has the potential to be quite large.

With this in mind, the client should know how the business relationship will be defined and how value will be assessed. It will help the client frame relevant questions and form answers if the client approaches the endeavor as one would approach any business project.

To the extent possible, there will be a clear set of goals and objectives, action plans with milestones, and a means of evaluating the outcome.

Time Commitments

The client and the coach will arrive at an understanding of the time commitments associated with the coaching. This will have been done in the contracting process as well as in the discussion on ground rules. Having a schedule and keeping to it are important aspects of the structure of the relationship. They also are good predictors of a successful outcome. In today's business environment, it is very easy to allow other events and meetings to crowd out coaching time. It is common for urgent things to take priority over important things.

Making changes in leadership or interpersonal style is the kind of task that requires continuity. That's why regular contact with the coach is important. Making these changes can be difficult, lonely work. Sticking to the schedule is a shared responsibility of the client and the coach, but slippage is much more often due to pressures on the client than on the coach.

Encourage the client to take responsibility for maintaining the integrity of the coaching schedule, just as he or she would for any other business obligation. Sometimes the coach serves as a kind of conscience, reminding the client to stick to the process. The client shouldn't let the coach become a nag!

If the client finds that time commitments cannot be kept, the client must have an open discussion with the coach. Maybe something is not working well in the relationship and the schedule slippage is a symptom of a larger problem.

Responsibilities to the Boss and to the HR Person

The client must recognize that the organization has made an investment of resources in him or her. The boss and you, the HR person, have agreed that the client's professional growth is important enough that time and money can be set aside for development.

What is the client's responsibility to them? What should the nature and frequency of the feedback to them be? Who should do it?

The answer to these questions varies depending on the client's level in the organization and on the client's relationships with you and the boss. There are no solid rules about this, but there are some good rules of thumb.

The organization has a vested interest in hearing the client's progress directly from the client. At the very least the client will want to give periodic updates to you and to the boss on how the coaching is proceeding. You and the boss will want to know if the relationship is working well, if each of you should be doing something to help it along, and if your observations could be helpful. It would be a good idea for the client to obtain a sense of your expectations concerning how often and in what modality you and the boss would like to be updated (voice, face-to-face, or email). If things aren't going well, then of course the client should speak up.

It is generally better for the client to keep the boss and the HR person up-to-date, rather than having the coach do it all. The coach's opinions are valued, of course, but what you really want to see is progress and growth in the client! In any case, it is best if the coach does not do all that work alone.

There may also be some differences in the extent to which clients communicate their progress to you, depending on their level in the organization. Clients at more senior levels are less likely to keep you and their boss up-to-date. They also may request that the coach keep conversations with others to a minimum. Although this may be more comfortable for the senior-level client, it doesn't necessarily serve the client's best interests. Clients at middle or first-level manager levels typically have less ability to operate with this kind of independence.

Coachable Moments

Some of the most valuable learning experiences come from "coachable moments." These are the occasions when the client recognizes that something important is happening that has to do with the focus of the coaching. If the client wants the coach's help, the client needs to speak up! Any coach will make time for a "coachable moment." Whether the client needs only a few minutes or a crisis is happening and the client needs more time, that's what coaches are for.

What do coachable moments look like? Crises are one example, but there are many others as well. It could be a situation that causes a peak in anxiety level—a sense that trouble is lurking. It could be an insight, an epiphany of some kind that says, "Now I get it!" It could be some negative feedback. It could be that an opportunity has come up to try out a new way of doing things.

The following is an example of a coachable moment:

> Don had been working with his coach, Sheila, for about two months. The coaching focused on two goals:
>
> 1. Helping Don move effectively into a "manager of managers" role, a task that resulted from his promotion just before the coaching started, and
> 2. Building a constructive—one hopes cooperative—relationship with Helen, one of his new peers.
>
> Sheila and Don had moved through the phases of contracting, assessment, and goal setting, and had settled into a rhythm of meetings every two weeks or so. Progress was being made on the first goal with his four direct reports. New boundaries were established; he moved his own style away from micromanaging to allow them a very significant degree of autonomy, a revised follow-up system was in place, and informal relationships were improving.
>
> But Helen remained aloof. She and Don were cordial to each other, but no real connection was being made. Don wasn't sure whether Helen resented him for some past misstep or just didn't trust him yet. Other hypotheses were discussed in the coaching sessions, most recently on

a Monday. Sheila and Don even sketched out possible scenarios for how Don could try to engage Helen in the areas where their work overlapped. Don was prepared to approach Helen with one of these conversations after the upcoming departmental meeting on Thursday.

On Tuesday of that week, about 10:00 a.m., Don called Sheila with a sense of urgency. He had received a call from Helen at 9:30 a.m. asking for a meeting that day. When he asked Helen what she wanted to talk about, her answer had to do with a need to borrow some of his key people for a few days to finish a major client assignment before the end of the week. Don and Helen agreed to meet at 2:00 p.m. that day. Don was looking for help from his coach on how to handle Helen's request.

Don wasn't sure what to do. Should he ask his boss? Should he ask for volunteers? Should he just tell his people to drop whatever they were doing so they could help Helen? He knew his people were stretched to get their own work done. He didn't like any of the alternatives.

Sheila recognized this as a "coachable moment." Sheila cleared her schedule so she could give Don the time he needed, which turned out to be more than an hour.

By noon, Don was clear about what he should do. He called a meeting of his direct reports. They developed a solution so that workloads were shared across organizational lines, priorities were maintained, and Helen got the help she needed. His 2:00 p.m. meeting with Helen, which included two of his direct reports, went smoothly. His relationships with his own people were honored and strengthened, and he built a bridge to Helen.

As you can see, coachable moments provide great opportunities for the client to practice new behaviors with the guidance of the coach. In your role as HR professional, it is important for you to know that when a client recognizes these chances for accelerated learning, the client can take a proactive role in dealing with them.

Summary

In this chapter, you have learned more about the client's role to help you achieve greater insight into what the client may be experiencing during the coaching process. The client's responsibilities to you, the HR person, and to the boss have been explained. You have been provided with some suggestions of what you can do to assist the client during the coaching engagement. Finally, you have gained a better understanding of the occasional "coachable moments" when a client has an opportunity for accelerated learning.

In the next chapter, you will learn more about the boss's role and how you can help the boss in providing feedback and support to the client.

7

What Is the Boss's Role?

In most situations, the client executive's boss is a central figure in the coaching activity. The boss's role may include identification of the need, initiating the coaching arrangement, offering detailed information, rewarding progress, and providing the budget for the coach.

Topics addressed in this chapter include the following:

- Creating the case for change

- Defining success

- Authorizing the coaching

- Identifying performance expectations

- Providing observations

- Assessing how well changes are going

- Helping the overall effort

Creating the Case for Change

Executives who are capable of making major business decisions aren't necessarily good at talking straight to their employees about what needs to change. Sometimes a coach arrives for a first visit to discover that the boss and the HR representative have agreed on what needs to change, but no one really told the client about it. Bosses are the ones who need to do this, in clear terms. The boss is the person who knows what good things might lie in wait for the employee who develops new competencies. The boss is the one who will need to take action regarding the employee who doesn't change a counterproductive style. The boss creates the case for change.

A related task is for the boss to become reasonably sure that what the employee is being asked to do is achievable. Is the boss comfortable that the changes can be made? Has the boss checked to see that the organization's culture or systems, or even his or her own way of managing, aren't the reasons why performance is hampered? If it is likely that the organization's way of doing business will foil attempts by the client acting alone to make the desired changes in performance, then thought needs to be given to other change strategies.

Defining Success

Following directly from the above notion, the boss is the one who will say "Well done" when the employee (with the coach's help) makes the desired changes. Or the boss might say "Not so well done." It's the boss's job to lay out the picture of success, at least in rough terms. The coach and client will massage the sketch, but they need something reasonably useful as a start.

Authorizing the Coaching

Whether or not the boss initiated the idea, it is the boss's decision to authorize the coaching. He or she is authorizing that the employee, the client, may use significant time and resources for this purpose. Along with you, the HR professional, the boss is declaring a vested interest in seeing the client's performance improve or his or her potential be more fully realized. The boss is expressing the belief that coaching is the appropriate way to go forward. You must hope that the boss also has a strong desire to see this improvement spread and have a positive effect on the functioning of a larger team, whether it is the client's direct reports, the client's peer group, or the boss's team as a whole.

Identifying Performance Expectations

From his or her position in the organization, the boss's perspective and insights are very valuable in providing the client with an understanding of what is required to be successful. The boss may have had discussions with the client that have led up to the decision to seek coaching. Certainly, at the point at which the client is ready to begin the coaching engagement, the boss's role in helping to define the standards for good performance is critical.

The boss can help to identify the client's performance expectations both for near- and long-term success. Using his or her knowledge of the strategic short-term and long-term goals of the business unit, the boss can engage in discussions with the client and coach to assist them in understanding these goals at a variety of levels.

- First, merely knowing and being able to define the business unit goals improves clarity of mission.

- At a second level, the client can obtain a view of how his or her role fits into the overall mission of the organization.

- Third, the client and the coach can define the behaviors needed for the successful attainment of the business goals. In light of the client's pattern of strengths and challenge areas and the strategic goals required by the organization, the coach and the client can focus on those behaviors that will have the greatest impact on success. This process occurs more easily if the organization has adopted a set of leadership competencies and if the boss can identify which behaviors are important for the client to demonstrate for successful job performance.

- Finally, the development of new behaviors can occur, not in a vacuum, but rather with an eye toward the practical application of these behaviors as they relate to the strategic goals of the business unit.

The overall outcome, therefore, has the potential to affect an entire system. It begins with the individual whose performance improves with coaching, progresses to a larger team, and eventually, if the goals have been met successfully, affects the overall functioning of the organization.

Providing Observations

As the client's supervisor, the boss can provide a unique viewpoint on the client's strengths and challenge areas. You will want to encourage the boss to take the time to offer thoughtful observations from his or her vantage point. This will pay off tremendously by enhancing the quality of the feedback given to the client. From the client's perspective, often it is the boss's feedback that has a special richness to it and carries more weight than feedback from other sources. Overall, you will want to encourage the boss to devote some time to thinking about what important points to make in his or her feedback and to schedule feedback sessions with the client.

Assessing How Well Changes Are Going

The boss's observations are needed not just at the start, of course. The boss should be talking from time to time with the coach and with the client.

The frequency of feedback is almost as important as the content of the feedback. When the boss observes changes in the client's behavior, it is very helpful to communicate these observations to the coach and to the client. Particularly early on in the assignment, it can be very rewarding for the client as well as the coach to know that favorable behavior changes are evident. Just how well the boss thinks the changes are going is a topic worth sharing with the coach, who is in a position to mediate this information with the client. If the boss does not see much change, then this fact is best communicated first to you and to the coach. There may be some reasons why behavior changes are not evident, and a three-way discussion may help to elucidate the reasons for this before involving the client.

If the boss thinks that the behavior changes are going well, the boss may want to be liberal with praise. This will reinforce the new behaviors and signal to the client and the coach that they are on the right track. In the long run, it is the boss's opinion that matters more than that of others, and any reinforcement from the boss is likely to have stronger effects than if the same words were to come from another source.

Helping the Overall Effort

How the boss communicates about the coaching effort can make or break its success. If the coaching is viewed as another way to accelerate the learning of new skills and behaviors, then it may more easily gain acceptance by the client and key stakeholders. If the coaching is viewed as a last-ditch remediation or a final desperate attempt, then the outcome may be seen as less hopeful and not worthy of the energy required to be expended. When coaching is viewed in a positive light, the motivations of the client, the coach, and the rest of the organization are focused on a successful outcome and it can become a win-win situation.

The boss's attitude about coaching is at the foundation of this matter. It's important that the boss believe in the employee's potential and in the efficacy of the coaching process. If the boss isn't a believer, it'll be hard for him or her to communicate in positive tones. If the boss thinks of it as a long shot, something that should be kept secret, the organization will pick up negative signals. If the boss is optimistic and sees coaching as an investment, that will help the overall effort.

Summary

In this chapter, you have learned more about the boss's role in the coaching process. This role may include identifying the need for coaching, initiating the coaching arrangement, providing information, offering feedback and rewarding progress, and providing the budget for the coach. You have gained an appreciation of the boss's pivotal role in creating the case for change and defining the standards for good performance. You have seen that you have a role in encouraging the boss to take the time to define the strategic goals of the business unit, to offer observations and feedback, and to reward the client's progress. Finally, you have seen the value in insuring that the boss's observations of the client's behavior changes are communicated to the coach and to the client.

In the next chapter, you will gain a greater understanding of the activities that are the coach's responsibility. This knowledge will position you as the liaison between the coach and the organization.

8

What Is the Coach's Role?

This chapter outlines important activities that are a coach's responsibility. It is intended as a very brief summary to help you know what's on a coach's mind as he or she goes about the coaching work.

Topics covered in this chapter include the following:

- Structuring the coaching process

- Communicating with organizational sponsors

- Setting boundaries for the coaching assignment

- Evaluating the impact of the coaching

- What coaches don't do

- When to discontinue coaching

Structuring the Coaching Process

In some large organizations, there is a formal coaching process managed by a professional with leadership development responsibilities. Outside coaches are expected to generally follow this established structure. Some of the large consulting firms also have relatively standardized approaches to how coaching assignments are structured.

In either case, there will be strong guidelines about how to do goal setting, assessment, action planning, implementation, and evaluation. Having this structure facilitates a cooperative, goal-oriented relationship. The steps outlined in Chapter 4 provide a good general approach to most coaching assignments.

Often, however, the coach has a good degree of flexibility and, therefore, also the task of spelling out how these steps will happen. This will be done at the outset of the engagement. The factors going into the coach's decisions include what the client is likely to need, what the organization and the HR professional are familiar with, and the coach's own favorite ways of working.

Some coaches prefer to be very explicit about steps and stages, while others are more comfortable with flexible arrangements. Some do a lot of interviews, by phone or in person, while others use 360-degree surveys or psychological tests. Some prefer to have regularly scheduled meetings. All good coaches reserve the right to do mid-process reviews to see whether the initial structure is working well.

The point is not so much *how* the coach works, but rather *how clearly* the coach is able to describe the process. The primary goal is to delineate what the process is, to take the mystery out of it so that others will know what's happening and can set their expectations accordingly. It's important to avoid assuming that all the stakeholders will automatically agree on what coaching is or should be. A clear structure also reduces the likelihood of "drift"—of a coaching relationship wandering off target or becoming just a supportive friendship.

Communicating with Organizational Sponsors

The coach is often thinking about how to communicate to the client's boss and with the HR professional. Even if weeks go by with no word to or from them, you are on the coach's mind. If you don't hear from the coach, feel free to give him or her a call. Coaches get busy too—new coaching clients don't arrive in the coach's life on a smooth schedule! Over a typical six-month assignment, a frequent pattern would be three or four conversations during the early stages, then perhaps a monthly check-in, and several longer conversations toward the end.

This communication is not just to see if all's going well. It is an opportunity to adjust the goals, to make sure everyone's expectations are realistic, and to solve problems. At times clients are overloaded, get sick, are promoted or transferred, or some other change occurs in the work setting. The coach and the HR professional need to share this kind of information.

The coach will want to hear your feedback regarding the boss's, the direct reports' and the peers' perceptions of the client. This is important data for calibrating the progress of the coaching assignment. It is also a major source of encouragement for the client who is engaged in the hard work of behavior change and may not receive this information directly.

Setting Boundaries for the Coaching Assignment

Coaches are also concerned with managing the boundaries of their relationships. Three kinds of boundary management issues are worth mentioning:

- Time stretch

- Scope creep

- Professional limits

Time Stretch

Time stretch happens when the amount of time needed to do an assignment expands beyond expectations. If the coach is billing for time spent, then the bills go up. If the coach is paid a one-time fee, then the profitability goes down. In either case, the work isn't coming to a completion in the timeframe initially established.

Experienced coaches will have a good sense of when the time-line is stretching out and will dig into the causes. It could be the client's workload, but it could be lots of other things too. If the assignment in fact turns out to be more difficult or a bigger one than was thought, recontracting is in order. If the cause is "resistance" of some kind, then it's up to the coach and the client to deal with it.

Scope Creep

Scope creep is a different matter. Coaching differs from other kinds of consulting in that the focus is entirely on one individual. It is obvious, of course, that the individual client is embedded in a web of relationships within the organization and elsewhere. It is not uncommon for some of those other people to become engaged in the client's coaching process in more than a passing manner.

Most often those other people are the client's direct reports and/or boss. What began as individual coaching slowly shifts into team building, conflict mediation, or some other form of professional service. The initial contract might have set limits about this kind of "scope creep," but most do not.

Depending on how extensive the additional work may be, the coach may simply incorporate it into the original assignment. However, the additional work may require a greater commitment of time or resources, as well as exceed the boundaries of the original agreement. Even if the coach does extend the assignment in this manner, it should be done with the informed agreement of all the stakeholders.

As a matter of good practice, we would encourage coaches to stick to the original deal. When that work is done, then a new proposal can be put forth to outline the additional work.

Professional Limits

Professional limits represent another kind of boundary that coaches should be thinking about. Coaches usually have a reasonably broad repertoire of competencies, but no coach knows how to handle every kind of client!

Good coaches are smart enough to know what they don't know and make referrals when those limits are reached. The HR professional could raise the topic of legal and medical limits with the coach by simply asking: "How will you know you have reached your boundaries?" Clients with significant personality issues may require a different coach than those who have skill development needs. Some personality issues shouldn't be handled by coaches at all, but by health care professionals. Some clients need coaches with experience in certain business arenas, such as technology or diversity.

Evaluating the Impact of the Coaching

How will you know whether or not the coach's work with the client is having an impact? Coaches want to be viewed as making a difference, as being helpful and worth the money they're being paid. They want to be "successful" for reasons of professional pride. They also have their "business development" hats on from time to time—they need good references and want repeat business.

Coaches and clients frequently talk about their subjective experiences of progress. "How's it going?" "Making headway?" "Sticking to the program?" They don't necessarily need to do a formal evaluation to know whether their joint effort has traction to it.

Nonetheless, it's good to get other opinions. Sometimes coaches will ask for this feedback from the HR person. There's also no reason why the HR person can't volunteer this information during the course of the assignment.

A best practice is for the coach, client, boss, and HR professional at the onset of the coaching to determine how success will be evaluated. Will there be periodic meetings among all of the parties or with a designated subset of them? How often will the coach provide progress reports and to whom?

As stated in Chapter 4, when a more formal evaluation is desired, there are a number of approaches that the coach and the client may want to take. If assessment data such as multi-rater feedback and survey data were collected at the start of the assignment, then a second round of assessment may be used for comparison between Time 1 and Time 2. This is recommended only if there has been sufficient time between the first and second data-collection efforts. Generally, a minimum of a six-month timeframe is needed to lapse between the first and second data collection in order for the client to initiate new behaviors and for those behaviors to actually be noticed by others.

Sometimes, qualitative methods, such as interviews, are sufficient to measure changes. These are especially effective if the interviews were also completed initially, so comparisons could be made between the themes emerging at Time 1 and Time 2.

Another source of evaluation of the impact of coaching is the action plan. If an action plan had been created as one of the steps in the coaching process, then the evaluation could center on how the goals in the action plan were completed.

What Coaches Don't Do

This next section really shouldn't be necessary, but unfortunately once in a while coaches are asked—explicitly or covertly—to take actions that are out of their proper domain. Sometimes the organization has a strong need for related services. Since the coach is already familiar with the issues in the organization and has established a level of comfort with others, there may be the tendency to ask the coach to do other work that is not appropriate to the coach's role or area of expertise. Some of this other work may involve the areas of supervision and employee selection.

Supervision

As we explained in Chapter 7, one of the most important roles of a boss is to create the case for behavior change. It is the task of the boss to tell the client what he or she needs to do differently in order to meet expectations. This is a supervisory task. The coach has no legitimacy on this matter, except as a messenger, which is an awkward role to be in. It is the boss who creates the case for change. The coach serves as the catalyst in helping the client to make it happen. The impetus for change must come from the boss during discussions with the client regarding the client's job performance and its impact on business results.

Employee Selection

Another inappropriate task for a coach is to evaluate the client as an employee to see whether the client is the right candidate for the job. Some coaches also do "psychological assessments" of candidates for jobs, and these assessments may have recommendations in them. However, asking a coach to determine whether the client is the right candidate for a job is not a good practice for both legal and practical reasons.

On the practical side, in a given coaching engagement, if the client has a sense that the coach is sitting in judgment on career issues, the coaching relationship is over. The bond of trust between coach and client cannot exist, and the client will, at best, be reluctant to share information needed for the coaching to be successful.

When to Discontinue Coaching

Coaching assignments don't always go smoothly. They can hit snags. When a snag is recognized, the HR professional has to get involved. It is also possible that the coach will not speak up and so the HR professional will have to step in. It is a good idea to have a meeting with the coach and the client.

Sometimes it's not just a snag, but a dead end. A coach might recommend that the coaching process be stopped, temporarily or permanently. This decision is usually made after a great deal of consideration. In discussions with the client and the HR person, an agreement might be reached that the client doesn't have a coaching problem, doesn't want to be coached, or that the chemistry just hasn't been good. These can be difficult truths that must be faced by the coach, the client, and the organization. If the coaching engagement has involved communication among the HR professional, the boss, the coach, and the client, then there will be no surprises. Although there may be the temptation to lay blame somewhere, all parties would benefit from resisting doing so. Sometimes the client just isn't ready or coaching is not appropriate (see Chapter 2). In these circumstances, it is important for all involved to practice listening and to keep an open mind.

A coach might suggest the client seek help of another type, in addition to what the coach is offering. Sometimes clients need help with building skills in areas pertinent to their jobs, such as making effective presentations, organizing and planning, or use of technology. Clients could benefit from the quick fix of experts in these areas in order to make more rapid progress. Sometimes clients have personal problems or crises that have to be handled separately but simultaneously with the coaching and require the services of an employee assistance bureau. The client may need to begin to resolve major life transitions involving divorce, death of a loved one, childcare, and eldercare. It may not make sense to stop the coaching while the transition is taking place. The situation may also require that you, the coach, and the boss handle the situation with extra sensitivity in order to protect the client. You may also want to give some attention to how to protect the organization, which had a need for something to happen in the coaching process. As you sort through your options, your challenge will be to find solutions that treat the client with dignity and respect and that also address the needs of the organization.

It is clear that what the coach should not do is terminate the relationship without discussion, notice, and good reason. The HR professional has a role to play by helping to set the tone that enables honest, candid discussion to take place.

Summary

In this chapter, you have learned more about the activities that are the coach's responsibility. These activities include structuring the coaching process, communicating with others in the organization, and setting the boundaries for the coaching relationship. You have gained some insight concerning how the coach values communication with you and the client's boss to be able to adjust goals and solve problems. You have also learned that the coach must manage the timeline allotted for the assignment as well as any work commitments beyond the original agreement. Your role in providing feedback to the coach regarding the perception of the success of the coaching assignment is very important. You have gained some insight into the importance of evaluating the success of coaching assignments and some approaches you might use. Finally, some reasons for terminating a coaching engagement have been provided so that you will know what situations will require your involvement in the decision to discontinue coaching.

In the next section, you will learn more about some special topic areas in which coaching has begun to play a larger role. Coaching has been helpful in accelerating learning when an executive is new to an organization (Assimilation Coaching), when formal classroom experiences are integrated with on-the-job experiences (Executive Development and Coaching), when executives must function across the globe (Multi-Cultural Issues), and when organizations wish to accelerate leadership development for a diverse workforce (Coaching and Diversity).

Section III

. . . .

Special Topics

This section addresses topic areas that have special relevance to coaching. As coaching has developed as a professional discipline, it has begun to play a larger role in those areas in which organizations have had a need to accelerate the employee learning process.

Chapter 9: Assimilation Coaching.   Organizations need to be able to assimilate new members quickly so that they can be as productive as possible in as short a timeframe as possible. Assimilation coaching helps a person adjust to a new organization by accelerating the learning process for newly placed individuals.

Chapter 10: Executive Development and Coaching.   Executive development programs have incorporated coaching as a way to help participants integrate the classroom experience with on-the-job experiences.

Chapter 11: Multi-Cultural Issues.   By applying cross-cultural coaching, organizations can help their executives function more effectively in different countries and cultures across the globe.

Chapter 12: Coaching and Diversity.   Having a diverse workforce gives an organization a competitive advantage. Coaching can be used very effectively to accelerate leadership development for an organization's diverse workforce.

In each of these special topic sections, the issue is defined and some explanation is provided about how coaching has been utilized to foster the adaptive functioning of both individuals and organizations. This section may be helpful for HR professionals who have broader responsibility in some of the areas related to these topics. It may also be relevant for clients who may be participating in executive development programs, who are dealing with diversity issues, or who are struggling with assimilation into a new organization. This section is also relevant for the clients' bosses, who, by virtue of their role, will also have a strong interest in seeing clients achieve success.

9

. . . .

Assimilation Coaching

A ssimilation coaching helps a person adjust or "assimilate" into
a new organization. Used most often at the executive level,
assimilation coaching can accelerate the learning process to enable
newly placed individuals and their teams to reach their business
goals faster.

Assimilation coaching gained in popularity during the 1990s as
more people moved laterally across companies as a result of the
increase in downsizings, consolidations, and mergers and acquisitions. Many organizations were faced with the task of "assimilating"
new executives from outside the company who were unfamiliar with
the culture. Having spent most of their careers at another company
or at several other companies, these executives had learned patterns
of behavior appropriate to a different corporate culture.

Frequently, the newly placed executives ran into difficulties very
early on—perhaps as early as the first three months. Within two
years, they were seeking employment elsewhere. These executives
frequently held upper-level positions, with responsibility for large
numbers of people and big budgets. Their failure to perform meant
greater risk and expense for the organization. Many savvy companies, therefore, realized that a coaching program could assist these
newly appointed individuals in making this important transition to
their new roles. It just made good business sense.

Common Issues

Some common issues are faced by new employees in a company. Assimilation coaching is designed to help an executive navigate during the early days of employment. Listed below are the kinds of questions (in four topic areas) that can form a basis for a discussion between a coach and a client during the assimilation process. It is important to recognize that the coach isn't expected to have all the answers. The coach knows that these questions should be asked and has ideas for how the client and coach, working together, can find the answers.

Understanding the Culture

- What is the mission and vision of the company and of your business unit?

- What's important and really counts here? What are the shared values and characteristics that comprise the organization's identity?

- How is performance measured? Is it done formally?

- How does the company recognize and reward people? How often?

- How does the communication process work? Is it very open, is there a lot of candor, or is it on a need-to-know basis? What are the preferred channels?

- In terms of marketplace success, what does the company emphasize? What truly drives the business?

Self-Awareness

- What excites you in this move to X organization? What concerns you?

- What expectations do you have for yourself and your team?

- How will you measure your success?

Perception of the Company

- How does the marketplace describe your company's image?

- What are some of the repeated stories, myths, legends, and heroes?

- What are some of the strong or unique traditions?

Role in the Organization

- What is your role in carrying out the organization's mission and vision?

- What are your business objectives for the next six months? One year? Two years or more?

- What makes you want to work here and stay?

- Whom do you need to influence in order to achieve your business results?

- How will you build support for yourself and your organization?

- To whom may you go to ask for help?

- What roadblocks or hurdles will you need to overcome in order to achieve results?

Use of Multi-Rater Feedback in the Assimilation Process

Once the client has been in the job long enough for people to know him or her sufficiently (perhaps six months or so), the coach may find it useful to provide feedback from assessments such as 360-degree feedback tools. This really helps the new executive understand how others such as the boss, peers, and direct reports have perceived and interpreted his or her actions during this initial but critical time period. It can also serve as a basis for many rich discussions with the coach and allows the executive to make behavioral adjustments that can contribute to a smooth transition and to long-term success.

10

Executive Development and Coaching

Executive development programs are specific events that are designed to accelerate leadership development in individuals and teams. They are designed to provide learning experiences of particular importance to the client's organization, such as strategic planning, change management, and team leadership. Clients may attend programs offered by universities, learning organizations such as the Center for Creative Leadership, or custom-designed programs coordinated by some combination of in-house training staff, external consultants, and educational institutions. Programs may range in length from one day to several weeks.

Business Events in the 1990s

Prior to the 1990s, it was commonplace for executives to take one or two weeks out of the office to attend an offsite training program. The idea was that executive development took place when the individual had the opportunity to study in a classroom setting with peers. The notion was similar to the experience of going away to college: management principles were best learned without the distractions of the mundane, everyday issues that arose in the office. Effective learning took place outside the office.

However, new pressures arose during the 1990s as businesses downsized. Influenced by business events in the 1990s, research on adult learning, and the effectiveness of coaching in long-term development, businesses have demanded changes in the framework of executive development programs.

As the premium placed on speed and efficiency increased and time pressures became more severe, most executives could no longer be away from the office for such lengthy periods of time. The formal classroom experience in many executive development programs had to be reduced drastically. In response to the driving forces behind organizational change (see Table 1.1), many organizations searched for executive development alternatives that would be less time-draining and perhaps even more effective.

New Insights into Adult Learning

Simultaneously, research on maximizing adult learning was consistently demonstrating that adults learn most effectively when formal training is accompanied by on-job experiences. The evidence brought forth from the Center for Creative Leadership showed that executives learn best when theoretical management concepts are brought to life through self-initiated, practical experiences encountered every day on the job.

When action plans were implemented following classroom training, executives were more likely to transform the lessons learned in the classroom into useful knowledge and wisdom, which enhanced their leadership ability.

As coaching has become more widely recognized as a method for enabling accelerated, personalized learning to take place, it has been incorporated into the design of many executive development programs. Participants view their follow-up coaching activities as a very valuable aspect of the learning experience.

Using Coaching to Increase the Effectiveness of Executive Development Programs

An effective methodology for combining formal classroom training with coaching occurs when the coach is an instructor or facilitator in the classroom portion of the program. When follow-up action plans are included in the program design, coaching in conjunction with the plans creates the continuity between the classroom and the on-job experiences.

Another helpful methodology occurs when the coach serves as a team facilitator during breakout sessions. Under this scenario, the role played by the coach is established early for the participants. At the same time, the coach gains an understanding of the program's purpose and principles and gets to know the participants. The coach also has the opportunity to see the interactions of the individual or the team. This information can prove to be very useful for the coach during the follow-up period, which may rely heavily on telephone rather than face-to-face interactions. The coach can use the insights gained from the face-to-face interactions to guide the individual and the team. If there is no opportunity to involve the coach in the classroom portion of the program, then it is important to find a way to provide the coach with the understanding of what had occurred during the initial program experience.

Advantages of Incorporating Coaching into an Executive Development Program

Coaching reinforces the learning objectives. When the program design includes the assignment of coaches to an individual or to a team, there is a greater likelihood that there will be a strong focus on the developmental objectives. As the team goes about its various activities, the coach can help to keep the team focused on the program's learning objectives or goals. The coach can point to particular events or situations that represent an opportunity to extract new learning points.

Coaching can help the individual achieve developmental goals. Sometimes the mere presence of a coach ensures that the development action plans created during the formal session will more likely be completed. Motivation can be enhanced when the individual knows that a coach has been assigned, and there is the presence of another party requiring accountability.

Coaching assists with complex, long-term learning. When the information to be acquired is relatively easy and less complex, then learning can be accomplished in a relatively brief timeframe. However, the more complex the desired knowledge, systems, or information, then the more time may be required for understanding and learning to take place. Multiple experiences under different circumstances may be necessary for the individual to recognize and ultimately achieve mastery. These experiences can be reinforced repetitively by the coach, whose role it is to generate discussion and reflection when needed.

The Importance of Adhering to a Process

A coaching process for executive development programs is just as important as one for individuals who are not in such programs. The steps in the process of incorporating coaching into executive development programs are similar to the steps to be taken in other coaching situations. They involve contracting, initial goal setting, assessment, action planning, and evaluation. This process can be followed even when there are large numbers of participants and multiple coaches, as is the case in executive development programs.

Contracting

The coaches must understand what the executive development program is about. It is critical to the success of the program to provide a document that outlines the purpose of the program and what is to be achieved during the follow-up period in which coaching services are provided. This document should also contain items related to timeframes, number of coaching hours, and estimated end dates.

Initial Goal Setting

The desired outcome of the development program and coaching process must be made very clear to all stakeholders. This is especially true when the coaching is done for a team of people. All members of the team have to have clarity about their purpose, the end goal, and the role of the coach.

Assessment

Many programs now include assessments that increase clients' self-awareness and enable them to better understand how they are perceived by others. It is very important that the assessments fit into the overall purpose of the program and that the clients understand the rationale for including them. The most powerful executive development programs enable clients to learn how they can achieve business results by increasing their efficacy as leaders.

Action Planning

Very often the coach is asked to assist the individual in implementing the action plans that have been generated in the formal classroom training. There is a greater likelihood that the action plans will be successfully implemented if accountability has been built into the process. Generating sound action plans that have been created by the individual ensures that the coaching process will result in successful business results.

Evaluation

The evaluation of the coaching process within an executive development program is made easier when the initial goal setting has involved the multiple stakeholders associated with the program. When the contracting and initial goal setting phases have been done well, then the criteria for evaluation can be clear. Some questions to ask the program participants include: Did the presence of the coach expedite the learning process? Were the business outcomes reached? Did the coach motivate the individuals to perform at their best?

In the future, it is likely that coaching will become more popular in the design of executive development programs. Program participants report that coaching adds value by integrating classroom ideas with practical, everyday knowledge. It fosters reflection and self-awareness and accelerates the learning process.

11

Multi-Cultural Issues

Global organizations need executives who can function well across different cultures. The challenges faced by expatriate managers are considerable, and organizations have discovered that coaching can assist executives in transitioning to new cultures. Often, expatriates are unfamiliar with the customs, cultures, and work habits of the local people. At the very least, they may feel uncomfortable in their new roles. As a result, they run the risk of making critical and costly mistakes. By applying cross-cultural coaching, multinational companies can help their managers enhance their global managerial and leadership skills and achieve desired business results.

Objectives of Multi-Cultural Coaching

The main focus of multi-cultural coaching is to help executives function more effectively in different countries and cultures across the globe. Coaching can help clients:

- To gain awareness and develop a deeper understanding of their own values, attitudes, behaviors, and communication patterns in comparison to those of the target countries.

- To identify key cultural differences and similarities and their application to work-related tasks.

- To develop and practice skills and techniques for dealing with cultural and business issues in an international environment.

- To accelerate cultural adaptation and improve their interactions with others from different cultures.

Cross-Cultural Coaching Clients

Cross-cultural coaching most often includes the development, orientation, and preparation of expatriates and their families before, during, and after foreign assignments. Cross-cultural coaching helps clients to develop self-awareness and specific skill sets that will enable the client to function in specific cultures. Furthermore, the clients are provided with guidance, follow-ups, and progress evaluations during their time abroad. This can be done either by a coach in the home country via phone or email or by a coach in the host country. Since spousal adjustment is critical for the expatriate's success, coaching may also be provided to the spouse as well.

Another critical transition occurs when the expatriate returns to the home country. Repatriation often causes anxiety and the need to readapt to one's own culture. In this case, the coach helps the client to become reacquainted with the procedures for conducting business in the home environment. Spouse coaching has gained more importance as the adjustment patterns of the family have been proven to contribute to an expatriate's success. Spouse coaching is often provided through groups. This allows the spouses to develop a support group and minimizes the isolation of being "different" in a foreign country.

Multi-cultural coaching can be useful in developing employees in headquarters' functions who are responsible for the management of, and the communication with, overseas operations. Coaching can help the executives gain some insight into the values and beliefs of others from different countries. This kind of alignment of human resources strategy with business strategy can lead to greater job satisfaction and productivity for each individual client and for the organization as a whole.

Cross-Cultural Coaching Methods

The choice of a coaching tool or a combination of methods depends, of course, on the client's needs. Members of certain cultures will find certain tools more acceptable than others. Furthermore, the tasks that the client needs to accomplish in a foreign assignment will vary, as will the required extent of interaction with locals. Also, the greater the similarity between the home and the host cultures, the smoother the transition is likely to be.

Regardless of the method chosen, it has to be remembered that training and development should not be seen as an event but as a continuous process, which in the case of expatriates starts before the foreign assignment and lasts until repatriation.

The following gives an overview of the most commonly used techniques employed in cross-cultural development efforts.

Simulations

Role playing: clients imagine themselves in situations presented by the coach and they act out simulated roles.

Case studies: clients are asked to develop a course of action for a particular problem. Solutions are then discussed with a coach (either in an individual or group context).

Instructional games/action planning: clients are given simplified real-life situations and they examine potential strategies that can be used to bridge cultural differences. The focus is on the development of interpersonal communication and business skills.

Programmed Instruction

Clients are asked to read about a cross-cultural encounter and choose an interpretation of what happened and why. Programmed instruction is designed to expose members of one culture to some of the basic concepts, attitudes, role perceptions, customs, and values of another. Most scenarios are based on critical incidents that are important to the respective culture.

Formal Instruction

Through lectures or tutorials, clients are given information about the expatriate adaptation cycle, the stages of adjustment, and the possibility of culture shock. Topic areas also include a geographical and historical briefing, security counseling, and language training.

The coach can help the client gain self-awareness and target the work-related tasks that are affected the most by cultural differences. The use of cross-cultural development tools can then help the client to learn new behaviors to maximize effectiveness in the new culture.

What to Look for in a Coach

A cross-cultural coach should:

- Be familiar with both the culture of the client and the culture of the target country

- Understand the implications of a different value system and behaviors in order to help the client use cultural differences to competitive advantage

- Be able to interact with people from other cultures

- Have some familiarity with a foreign environment in order to anticipate the challenges the clients are likely to encounter

- Be willing to understand the client's culture and see his or her point of view

- Be skilled in understanding non-verbal behaviors, because in an international context, coach and client often do not share the same first language so the accurate interpretation of non-verbal behaviors takes on greater importance

Conclusion

Because the cross-cultural components add a level of complexity not present in other coaching situations, it is very important to tailor a development program that addresses the needs of each individual as well as the business needs of the organization.

Cultural adaptation and communication problems are one of the greatest challenges facing executives in global business. However, an overseas experience can be an unparalleled opportunity for personal growth and learning. Cross-cultural coaching can make a valuable contribution by helping to make the cross-cultural experience unique and personally satisfying for the client as well as rewarding for the organization.

12

Coaching and Diversity

Diversity in the workplace is often referred to as the differences among a group of people—typically, such differences as race, ethnicity, cultural background, gender, age, class, or religion—working together in an organization. Diversity not only reflects the varying demographics among employees in an organization, but also the wide range of abilities, values, expectations, and personalities among those people.

Sharing different perspectives, generating innovative ideas, and offering creative solutions are some of the benefits of diversity in the workplace. However, diversity may also pose a significant challenge if employees have different opinions or values that can lead to exclusion, miscommunication, and even conflict. Overcoming these challenges and leveraging the benefits of diversity requires having an organizational culture that values an inclusive work environment.

The Role of Coaching

What role might coaching play in helping an organization leverage diversity? Employing coaches within an organization with a diverse workforce may serve several purposes. In addition to developing the leadership skills of a diverse workforce, it can help the organization demonstrate a commitment to diversity, foster retention of talent, and maintain its competitive advantage. The points made in Chapter 2 on "when coaching is appropriate" and "how a coach helps" are certainly relevant here.

Questions Coaches May Ask

Well-trained and experienced coaches make it a priority to identify and understand differences and similarities between them and their clients early in the coaching relationship. Knowledgeable coaches who have experience working with diverse clients ask questions to explore the best strategies to use to meet client needs. Some questions a coach might ask in the early stages of the coaching relationship follow:

- What should I know about you and your strengths/experiences/challenges/perceptions, and so forth that will help me coach you more effectively?

- What is the best way for me to help you achieve your goals and provide you feedback?

- What are your expectations about the coaching relationship?

Use of Assessment

As one of the steps used in the coaching process (see Chapter 4), asking questions or using assessments may be very valuable tools for use with diverse clients. The multi-rater feedback process enables clients to gain a clearer picture of how others see them and can foster an increase in self-awareness. Creating such a feedback-rich environment can accelerate the learning process and make significant contributions to the development of talent in the organization.

Selection of Coaches for a Diverse Population

When selecting coaches to work with a diverse client population, HR professionals may look for a coach who:

- *Has knowledge and experience with diversity issues.* Does the coach show an interest in diversity, awareness of relevant issues, and willingness to learn about the particular challenges different employees face? What can the coach tell you about his or her experiences with diverse clients? How has the coach helped clients identify strategies that emphasize their best attributes and how these attributes fit within the organizational culture?

- *Avoids making assumptions.* Does the coach demonstrate awareness of his or her own beliefs and perceptions—whether about certain populations or about the coaching process itself? How does the coach acknowledge that there are differences as well as similarities among different people? How does the coach consider how differences between the client and the coach might impact the coaching relationship?

- *Communicates effectively.* How does the coach promote communication flow in the relationship when there are differences in communication style between him- or herself and the client? How does the coach listen, observe, and ask questions to determine the best coaching style to use with the client?

Role of the HR Professional

It is clear that coaching has an important role to play in accelerating the learning among a diverse workforce. For many HR professionals, valuing diversity is a key HR strategy for their organizations.

As an HR professional, you may have a pivotal role in helping your organization create a culture that values both diversity and leadership development for all employees. At the very least, teaming with other HR people who may have direct responsibility for diversity or leadership development may enable both you and the organization to arrive at more effective and strategic HR solutions for your workforce.

Section IV

. . . .

In the Words of Clients

This section contains stories that were written in retrospect in the words of various individuals to provide first-hand accounts of the experience of coaching. The names of the actual clients have been changed to maintain confidentiality. The purpose for including these stories is to provide readers with a better understanding of what clients may experience in a small sample of coaching situations and how coaching contributed to their executive development.

At the beginning of each story, there is a brief narrative that "sets the stage," telling about the client and the situation.

Maria's Story

. . . .

Maria was a systems designer who advanced to a role requiring her to manage the redesign of a major portion of her company's customer-related software. Her work involved upgrading the company's area of competitive advantage. She worked with all major internal users as well as customers and contractors. She met her coach when she was about thirty-six years old.

Her story is a good example of how a sensitive manager can help an employee with timely coaching. In retrospect, a number of coachable "issues" were present in Maria's life at that time:

- *A new role in a very ambiguous environment, in a fast-paced financial organization*
- *A transfer from London to the U.S., with little or no social support available either at work or personally*
- *Her history of rapid advancement but without feedback or clarity about her strengths or limitations*

Maria rightly identifies the issue of cultural differences that she (and everyone else) underestimated. This was true for a woman moving from one English-speaking environment to another and who had previously lived on the Continent and spoke other languages fluently. One can only imagine the gaps that others need to bridge when they cross much bigger cultural distances with less personal international experience.

. . . .

Having worked for several years in the London office of a U.S. company, I was fortunate enough to be given the opportunity to expatriate to the head office in the U.S. This meant being provided with a one-way ticket, help with accommodations, and introductions to the people I needed to meet (and win over). After months of operating within a group whose authority was not established and whose role was ambiguous in the company's unstructured hierarchy, I was in professional distress—unfocused, unsure of my position, and ready to quit trying. As a perfectionist and a high achiever, my self-confidence was ebbing, as I did not know how to progress in such an unstructured environment. Recognizing that we were collectively in danger of failing, my manager secured for me the services of an executive coach he knew, liked, and trusted and who already had a relationship with the company. Several things are important here— my manager spotted my problem, recognized he could not fix it, and was prepared to donate the budget and time.

Although I had no prior coaching experience, I had a vague idea of what I needed, and that was a basic survival guide. Not just survival in the company I was in, but in corporate America in general. My English culture made it initially hard to accept that I would benefit from seeing a corporate psychologist, but I had little to lose and the early tests such as Myers-Briggs were painless and confidence-building. As time went on, my coach—my best buddy, arch supporter, and personal challenger all in one—got me to look at the company differently and also, more importantly perhaps, to look inside myself in order to adapt. Self-examination is uncomfortable, but there was a constant reminder—backed up by the psychological tests—that I was smart, worth something. My coach knew my company intimately, and this understanding of both the environment and myself was critical to our success.

I think I learned an enormous amount in a considerably short space of time. In the competitive environment where I worked for fifteen years, nobody had pointed out my skill set, and praise came in the form of a bonus. I had advanced to a prominent position without really having a good understanding of what I was good at and why. As we covered the political, bureaucratic, social, and cultural identity and issues of my company, and my operation within it, I discovered three things:

- First, how to maneuver in my environment by finding sponsors who would fight in my corner where I could not. This allowed me to navigate better without hanging my hat on anyone's particular political peg.

- Second, that the problem was not me. It was the combination of me + the job + the environment.

- Third, never to underestimate cultural differences.

It has been four years since I first met my coach, and the benefits I got from coaching are part of my psyche. I went on to manage a team of people and was keenly aware how the fit of people and environments is crucial to success. My own coaching made me a better manager, as I assumed an obligation to my staff to help them progress personally as well as meet corporate deadlines, that is, mentoring as well as managing. I take pride in this success as I still get calls from those who worked for me over two years ago, looking for a little extra insight. In a harsh corporate environment where personal progression and any form of corporate training or career planning has dropped off the radar, it is up to the managers to help their teams as best they can, but this is not necessarily an in-built skill, let alone a job requirement.

Coaching was a huge success for me, but equally importantly, I tip my hat to my own manager, who identified that I needed help before I did, knew that he did not have the skill set to help, but knew someone who could and was prepared to fund it. Also critical was the personality fit with the coach, and her knowledge of the environment I was operating in. My coaching was finite, but several years on now, my relationship with my coach remains respectfully close. I honestly think that if I hadn't had this opportunity, I would have packed and gone back to London.

Howard's Story

Howard is one of a half-dozen members of senior management in a closely held technology company. On the surface, management's concerns were simple enough: get Howard to set and maintain his priorities. Howard's very significant talents were being used by everyone else in the company to their benefit but not to Howard's and not really to the organization's best interests. Howard enjoyed being included in everything. He knew he should be more focused but couldn't bring himself to work that way.

Howard's company is not a frequent user of coaching. His HR director pressed the case in this instance, since she could so clearly see the value of the service for this very important employee.

I started to work with a coach not by choice. Or rather I should be more specific and say, "Not by *my* choice." In fact, coaching per se never even occurred to me!

I should explain.

It is absolutely true that I have known about my need to get my work life organized. I have thought about using an "organization consultant" a few times. I even had one call me. But I never followed up on this. I didn't think it belonged on my top priority to-do list.

When I look back on this now and try to remember why I resisted some simple steps, two things come to mind. First of all, it seemed gimmicky to me. Organization specialist, consultant—whatever—just seemed like a waste of time. (The irony is not lost on me.) After all, if I needed tips on organizing, our HR department was always posting helpful hints at the bulletin boards by the elevator. I just needed to copy some of this stuff down and follow it. But the second reason is the real reason. I believed that my value to my company was greatly enhanced by my perceived ability to engage on dozens of topics, projects, and tasks all at the same time. If things fell through the cracks, I would pick them up later. If people got upset at me for not getting back to them in a timely way, well, I felt I was making good choices about what I concentrated on. They would have to wait.

So it's easy to see how these two reasons were really only one. I didn't seek coaching help of any kind because I couldn't conceive that I needed any.

Well, the owners of my company—my bosses—thought differently. For a long time, they tried to offer me help, guidance, assistance, and some management to get me pointed in the right direction. But, to be frank, this is not the forte of my bosses—management, that is. And I was mostly left to figure this out on my own. And here's the paradox. Because of my talents, I kept moving up the executive management path at my company. I was trusted with more and more decision making as well as more and more important projects. Unfortunately, this has the reverse effect on my performance in their eyes. Late last year, I was called to a meeting with the COO. He gave me the bad news. As soon as he finished with me, I was handed the "letter" from the company founder (the majority owner), which spelled out in great detail his great disappointment with my performance.

Luckily, they held out one carrot to me. They wanted me to start executive coaching. They believed in me deeply. They believed that I had the talent and intellect to achieve great things for my company. They also believed that I needed outside help since they couldn't seem to affect me like they wanted to. I met with the head of HR, who said she had just the person in mind that she thought could help me. And, just like that, my executive coaching experience began.

Needless to say, I believe that my overriding thought as we started was "caution." The first couple of sessions were extremely important to me. My company was paying for this, but I was the client. How was this supposed to work? Exactly what could I say to the coach? What could we talk about in confidence and what would be reported back to the company? She understood my anxiety and addressed this topic head on. As I look back on it now, without gaining my trust in this area, I don't believe there would have been any effective coaching at all.

As I write this piece, I try to think of all of the ways that she has helped me. And I try to put them in order of importance (yes, it's true; I think this way all of the time now). I think there were a few key areas that are the most important. First of all, after meeting with my bosses, my coach was able to reassure me (over and over) that I was considered a valuable senior employee in every sense of the word. Like most things, I believe that the coach intuitively understood that when your world is rocked, as mine was, reassurance is never in short supply. As we got to know each other more (and she was clearly more open with me), she was even more specific about this assurance issue. By telling me that, in her opinion (which by then I placed great faith in), there were no underlying, unstated negative undertones of any kind about my bosses' belief in me, I think she provided me with an important building block.

She once said to me that sometimes she has clients who just need a little nudge and that I personified that type of client. Certainly my wake-up letter from the owner made me look deeply inside myself. My lack of focus on the most important issues at work has been an overriding theme of my entire business career. I have always known this instinctively. But it had never threatened my career before. So I didn't need the coach to explain this to me. What I did need was help learning how to focus.

I think that she did this in two ways. First, there was the tangible way. I made a list. I went over it with her many times and every couple of months I presented this list to my bosses. But the more important part was less tangible. We talked about the creation and maintenance of the list. By talking and discussing how things get on the list, off the list, and move around the list, she helped provide me with some practical ways to organize my thoughts about what was most important to the company. There is no magic trick to this. It is simply a matter of reorienting my perspective. Frankly, it has been not only fun, but also a relief. It is a heavy burden to carry a list with thirty to forty projects, each in some state of "unfinished."

Finally, I think that she has given me a very realistic and positive outlook about both my company and my career. Her business experience certainly allows her to have business opinions about these large endeavors that I am involved in at my company. And, since we work with very large, well-known clients, she can bring real-world business opinions about them to our discussions as well. Her professional experience also allows her to teach me about the kind of company I work for and what that means to me. I feel much more able to have an objective view about both these areas as a result of my meetings with my coach.

Certainly my relationship with her changed over time. I do think of her as somewhat of a confidant now. There isn't anything that I wouldn't say to her about how I am feeling about work issues. Likewise, I think that her relationship with me has changed as well. Certainly, professionally, she knows that I am ready for direct talk on any subject. This makes it easier to cover pretty much anything.

Am I done with executive coaching? I hope not and, luckily for me, my bosses are so happy with the "new" me that they are happy to pay. I feel that, with additional time, the type of focus and discernment that I exercise with my coach's help can become second nature to me.

David's Story

. . . .

David's coaching is typical of long-term assignments at the very senior level. David was a prominent member of top management, reporting to the CEO. Both men were still in their thirties. David's concerns were with his own effectiveness and continued development. He requested the coaching. In this assignment there was essentially no further relationship between the coach and either HR or the CEO.

During a time of difficulty in a new role, I decided coaching might be a way to help me be more effective at my job. At the time I had been a manager for six years, and I was twelve years into my working career. I was aware of the idea of coaching because one of my colleagues had found a relationship with his coach to be quite useful to him. I did not really understand what a coaching relationship entailed, but I figured it could only help me.

After I discussed it with the HR department in my company, they brought me three candidates to choose from. I liked two of the three. One of them was a clinical psychologist, and one was a businessman who had sold his well-known company some years before. I chose the coach with the business background because I thought he would have more of a connection to my job and me.

Before I started the coaching I was not sure what to expect. Would a coach see things I did not see? How would he advise me on what I should do to be more effective? Would he know enough about the issues I faced to help guide me in making things better?

I began our relationship by using my coach as a sounding board for everything I had questions about: issues I was having with my peers on the executive committee, issues with people who worked for me, issues with building or revamping parts of my organization, et cetera. During our first few meetings my coach asked me many questions so he could learn about my history, my style, my issues, my responsibilities, and me.

Over time, my coach came to understand my company's organizational issues and politics. This was critical, as the organization seemed to be in a constant state of flux. For our first three years together, I had a new set of responsibilities each year, and the makeup of the senior management team, of which I was a member, had about 30 percent turnover. It was a very volatile environment internally. This made it difficult to focus on my core responsibilities, which included being responsible for sales as well as new product development in certain market segments. There always seemed to be major organizational issues to contend with, and having a coach at my side was invaluable in dealing with them.

One of the first things I realized about a coaching relationship was that a coach helps people with similar issues no matter what job they might have. Coaching is not about helping with the "results" aspects of a job; it is about the "management" aspects of a job. A coach can help anyone with being a better manager, learning to communicate more effectively, or dealing with difficult situations. My coach helped me with various parts of my job as it related to leading, organizing, and managing a business unit. He did not help me with my role of generating revenue, new products, et cetera.

In retrospect, one of the most interesting aspects of our relationship is that the focus of my coach was not about helping me with *what decisions* I made; it was about the process of *getting to* the decision. For example, when I needed to create an organizational structure for a newly formed business unit, I had some difficult people issues, such as which of two peers would become the other's boss. My coach did not suggest who should get what job; he simply helped me ask and answer the questions that led to me not just making a decision, but being comfortable enough with the decision that I was able to sell it well internally. Over time, this process became ingrained in me and I learned, to some extent, to ask myself those same types of questions.

One of the great benefits the relationship brought to me was simply having someone to talk to about certain sensitive issues that I could discuss with few if any people within my company. At the same time I was beginning the relationship with my coach, my long-time boss was in a tough situation and I did not get to speak to him very often. Having a coach gave me someone I could bounce things off of, who could understand the issues within the company, and could understand where I was coming from and help me see my options and plan a course of action.

My coach was particularly helpful with what I call the "Am I crazy?" questions. I think we all face situations that, for one reason or another, don't make sense. Whether it is the actions of others, the inability to get what seems like an appropriate project or course of action approved by the CEO, et cetera. Typically these are the situations you can only bounce off your own team, who would usually agree with you. When you are on your own, you question your thinking and decision making; "Am I crazy?" Having my coach to help me analyze these situations was invaluable, whether he gave me a plausible explanation that I had not thought of or simply said, "No, you are not crazy. This does not make sense." Getting this feedback from someone I respected, who understood the people and issues I was involved with, and who had credibility as a businessperson gave me tremendous comfort.

My relationship with my coach developed over time into one that was very comfortable and casual. We developed two main patterns of working. One was focused on attacking specific problems and issues. I would describe a situation and possible solutions and use my coach both as a sounding board and as someone to help me work through to an answer. He did a good job making clear that his role was not to tell me *what* to do, but to help me learn *how* to use a consistent process to analyze issues and deal with them. The other thing we did together was to work on more project-oriented issues, generally around organizational management issues. For example, when I was restructuring a new business unit and had a list of ten major issues to be dealt with over a number of weeks or months, he was there to help me set up the process, time line, et cetera. He also worked with me on a number of "offsite" meetings over the years where I would be working with my management team, or a particular business unit, on a particular set of issues. Having him actually attend, and even help run some of these meetings, was quite useful both for his expertise and for the inside look it gave him into my issues and my staff.

One thing my coach did not do was to act as a cheerleader for me. I noticed he rarely gave me more than a subdued "good job" when I was telling him about one success or another. I remember realizing this and thinking that a good coach must remain objective. If he were always on my side, like my boss or certain employees, I would not have gotten nearly as much out of the relationship.

I liked it when he would critique me. I rarely received the type of constructive, and instructive, criticism intended to help me improve my skills. I realized that for the first time in my career I had someone who was focused on giving me constructive criticism in order to make me a better executive, and that was his only job. While there were many people who had criticized various aspects of my work over the years, there is a big difference between straight criticism and objective constructive criticism. Most of what I received over the years was simply criticism.

The seminal coaching moment of our relationship was one time a few years into our relationship. My coach and I were having a meeting in my office. I received a call I had to take because of some sort of problem. I remember talking the fellow on the phone through a solution for the problem, while my coach sat and watched me "in action." I hung up the phone very proud of myself for having so quickly and easily solved the problem. Then my coach commented on how *I* had just solved the problem, rather than having helped the person involved figure it out himself. Ouch! I knew better, even preached this to my own people, but here I was playing the hero as problem solver rather than being a good manager. If I had done some teaching instead, maybe the next time this person would be able to solve the problem on his own.

I still think about that situation often, constantly pushing myself not to provide answers, but to help others find them and, more importantly, to make it a repeatable process. Sitting on my desk is a card that reads, "Don't Preach, Ask Questions."

The lessons I took from my coaching relationship have lived on in my new career as a consultant in the financial service industry. While I am hired mainly to help organizations with sales management and product strategy issues, my clients get a "coach" thrown in as part of the relationship. I am particularly careful to focus on helping others learn how to solve their own problems and to teach them to create decision-making processes rather than trying to solve all of their problems.

Charlie's Story

*Charlie's story is a complex one. In this case the client is a sophisti-
cated, successful HR executive who is comfortable asking for
and using help. He reached out for a coach at a time of transition in
his life.*

What led you to use coaching?

I came to a place in my life where I knew I needed to step back and
completely evaluate the appropriateness of my life trajectory. I had
spent twenty-five years in corporate settings and I knew that yet
another corporate setting was not going to offer me the kind of life
that I was seeking.

I have always believed that one lives best when one lives dialog-
ically. These kinds of journeys are best NOT taken alone. The challenge is to find the right journey partner at the right time to
accompany you on through that space.

What had been your history with coaches?

Having spent twenty-five years in human resources consulting and at
the top of HR functions for four global companies, I have been both

a coach and a hirer of coaches. Early on, I was an advocate for coaching in several environments and quite successfully used coaching to help individuals work through developmental moments. Sometimes the coaching was created by a crisis . . . sometimes the coaching was to prepare someone for greater responsibility.

As a result, I came to know more than one hundred executive coaches in the U.S. and Europe . . . understanding their differing philosophies, approaches, tools, and relationship management skills. In my senior HR role, it was often my task to play "matchmaker" between coach and coachee, making my best judgment about best fit vis-à-vis temperament, style, skills, and desired outcomes. As with all human ventures, I experienced both success and failure in those matches. I generally have become quite cynical about the world of coaches. Virtually anyone can and is hanging out a shingle as some kind of coach.

How was the decision made to use a particular coach?

Throughout my professional life, I have always maintained a personal board of directors. This is a small group of very smart and effective people to whom I turn for a sanity check on my life plans. The coach I selected has been on my personal board for twenty years. He is organizationally savvy, knows me well, has high standards, insists on intellectual integrity, and is not afraid to push me into uncomfortable/developmental spaces.

What feelings were most clear to you as you started the coaching process and as time went on?

I knew that I was going to have to temper my need for quick analysis and a life-long habit of being so goal-directed that I would race to find the problem to be fixed. I know that I had to become comfortable with the ambiguity of the journey. My coach helped me do that by keeping me focused on the goals of coaching, not the specific outcomes.

As time went on, I relaxed into the role of true journeyer—allowing time for reflection, writing, and the emergence of inner voices. This required my coach's assistance in muting many of the old "tapes" and assumptions that I held about the word and work. As an ENTP, I am prone to tangential thinking. My coach allowed those tangents but knew when to rein them in when they were becoming counterproductive.

How would you describe the relationship with the coach? Did it change over time? Where did it end up?

While I had known this man for many years, our relationship moved to a new place right from the start. He generously shared insights from his own journey that allowed me to anchor my own experience. Since I walked into the experience with complete trust, that was not an issue.

His knowledge of my past turned out to be a useful thing. In my coachee mode, I was in a state of wanting to dismantle/forget everything that had happened to me in the first half of my life. He was able to help me confront the past in a productive way so I could come to terms with it.

In the same way, he knew that I could get caught up in the excitement of new ideas and was in a mode of devouring virtually everything I read. Again, he set parameters here to keep me in focus.

Initially, he asked excellent open-ended, exploratory questions. As we moved though the process, I began to generate more and more of my own questions and answers that he would help me dissect to glean the essence from both. In the end, our relationship is not fundamentally changed. Yet, I know him and he knows me on a much deeper level. I think we simply became even better friends. But at no time was the friend/coach line breached. The next time I feel that I require the benefits of a coach, I would not hesitate to work with him again.

What was most helpful?

This is not in any particular order, but the items below stand out as being most helpful:

- Excellent questions, evoked by active listening and his ability to read between the lines of what I was saying.

- His ability to connect unrelated dots in a mental picture that I might not be able to see.

- His ability to directly (yet respectfully) challenge my beliefs, assumptions, and values, drilling to the root sources of each, determining whether they still added value, were correct for me, or needed to be let go.

- He provided timely, immediate, and helpful feedback. The process was iterative . . . and we wasted very little time.

- He was open to my learning style, which is to reflect, write, and offer reams of paper for him to read. He allowed me to do this, and I could always count on a very thorough critique of what I had written. This allowed me to be very concrete about what I was thinking and feeling . . . and allowed him to check in and understand what I was thinking and feeling.

- He is a wonderful reframer of issues. Often, my lenses just needed a slight correction to see an issue more clearly.

- He often raised questions or issues that I had never considered or was blind to.

- He brokered introductions to others who added their personal life stories to my own assessment. This helped me significantly expand my own sense of the realm of the possible.

- He focused me to balance both action and reflection.

- He never tried to play the role of being my "shrink." We clearly delineated life planning issues from psychological ones.

- He taught me to become comfortable being on a journey where the destination is unknown. Also, I learned to embrace ambiguity on a level that I had not previously.

- He held me to my stated goals and mission, not allowing me to cave to time pressure or convenience or a new idea or relationship that seemed like "the answer."

- He refused to allow me to "should" myself.

- He never lost sight (nor allowed me to lose sight) of the systemic impact of my thinking and ideas. We always looked broadly at family, work, and life systems and implications.

- He offered questions and pathways, not solutions. He remained present and awake . . . allowing me to do the same.

- When I was really running amok, he did not hesitate to be instantly redirective.

What did not prove to be useful?

We are at very different seasons in our lives. Sometimes his sense of "been there, done that" caused him not to resonate with my excitement over an idea.

As with every human interaction, we each were (from time to time) the object of the other's projections.

Are you aware of using the benefits of the coaching in your work today?

Coaching senior executives is a part of my life's work. His model has greatly improved my effectiveness.

Are you using the benefits from the coaching in your continuing development?

I continue to access a personal board of directors. However, as a result of this experience, I have changed the nature of that group. I am surrounding myself with more divergent and better thinkers.

Carter's Story

Carter is the eldest of the people who contributed stories. He was in his late fifties at the time of coaching. The coaching assignment shifted focus several times over about eighteen months. As you'll read, he elected to leave the company and make strides to take charge of his life in its next phase—whatever that would turn out to be. Along the way he encountered and dealt with several very personal issues, such as his negative feelings about a place he had thought of as "home" for thirty-five years.

Also in this story are Carter's reactions to several "techniques" used by his coach—the writing of "books," which he found useful, and the collecting of data by himself from friends, which he decided not to do. Much of coaching is trial and error for both coach and client!

I was at a stage of life and career when I needed to make a change. I was leaving my company after thirty-five years and was not sure what I wanted to do. I started meeting with my coach about six months prior to the official sponsorship of the coaching by the company. He was well-known in the company, had experience coaching some of my colleagues, and had a good reputation. I did not seek a coach, but I sought out the idea of coaching.

After the initial period of six months of coaching conversations, I made a decision about leaving my company and coaching was included as a part of my "departure" package. That was my first time having a full-time coach; I had someone work with me on presentation skills, but that was quite different.

At the time I had a lot of difficulties looking at myself objectively and identifying my strengths and weaknesses. Only a few years after coaching did I realize that I was dealing with a lot of anger toward my company at the time. The anger was controlling and directing me. It was important to move out, and that's the decision I had to come to terms with.

In the course of the coaching, we used some tests in the beginning and the end that were somewhat useful, but the most important realizations happened during my conversations with him. I think that initially the assignment was difficult for both of us. I threw a lot of information at him and vented. It was hard for me to separate the facts from the feelings. My coach got me to talk about my strengths and weaknesses. He held the mirror up and helped me focus on what my interests are. He did not make the decisions for me; he helped me make my own decisions.

I needed to wipe the slate clean, accept things as they are, and move forward, think about the next step in my life and what it is going to look like. One of the ideas that he came up with was helpful for me in sorting through my decisions. He talked about three books in your professional life: the first one is your training and preparation, book 2 is your career, and book 3 is what happens after you move on to other things and realize you have to do something for the next twenty or twenty-five years of your life. I started writing book 3 during my coaching.

I don't honestly know whether I may have elected to leave the company had it not been for coaching. I could have stayed on. I am generally risk averse. I may have stayed on and drifted. The idea of drifting is something else that came up during the coaching. It was liberating to learn that it is sometimes O.K. just to drift and not have to find answers for a while.

At some point midway through the coaching I had a conversation with one of my colleagues who asked me why I was getting all the "lousy" assignments and a light bulb went on. I also realized that corporations are not always nice places to be in and decided to move on. This would not have been possible had the coach not set the foundation for my decision during the coaching conversations we were having.

His style appealed to me as it was not hugely psychological; it felt like having a guide. He is friendly, an experienced professional, someone with great integrity and great values. A real person, who is not taking you through a psychological method but someone to talk to. You don't end up dissecting yourself; rather you look at yourself in a different light.

One of the things that I sabotaged during the coaching engagement was an assignment he gave me. I was to talk to five people about my greatest achievements and failures. I was afraid to do it. We often don't give good feedback face-to-face. You tend to downplay weaknesses and shortcomings. Some people are able to make that work, but I was not going to do it.

He and I talked about the options that lay ahead of me. I don't have to duplicate what I was doing all my professional life and sit on another board. I could do extensions, do a master's degree in arts or history, or, as I chose to do, invest heavily in the Internet start-up. It was 2001 and things did not go as well as I planned but I took my risks.

Section V

· ·

Reproducible Resources and Forms

We provide a description below of what the forms in this section contain and we describe how they can help you in your work of finding executive coaches for your clients.

Common Coaching Situations. This resource is a summary list of some common categories of coaching clients based on the challenges they are encountering. Once you have identified which of your clients might fall into a particular situation, you can see what types of things they need to achieve in that particular circumstance. The "Considerations" column provides you with some relevant questions you will need to ask in the selection of a coach and the use of a coaching process to address the developmental needs of the individual. This list will be useful when you do succession planning or other reviews in which you need to assess the talent in the organization and determine developmental needs. See Chapter 2 for a fuller explanation of when coaching is appropriate.

Questions for an Interview with a Prospective Coach. This list of questions and potential responses may be used when you want to interview a coach to determine whether the coach's experience is a good fit for the coaching assignment. You can pick and choose which questions to add to an already existing interview protocol. You may also want to use the questions in your conversations with a coach as a way of getting to know the coach better. See Chapter 3 for a better understanding of the practical issues involved in selecting a coach.

Agenda Items for an Initial Discussion Among HR Professional, Client, Boss, and Coach.   This list of questions may be used in a first meeting between these parties to help set expectations for the coaching engagement. Refer to Chapter 4 for a discussion on an initial four-way meeting.

Sample Agreement for Coaching Services.   This is a sample of a relatively more formal agreement that describes the scope of coaching services to be performed by the coach. You may wish to use an agreement similar to this one as an addendum to a contract created by your legal department. Refer to Chapter 4 for a discussion on the initial contracting step in the coaching process.

Sample Action Plan.   This form provides an example of an action plan that begins with a goal, measures used to indicate the successful attainment of the goal, actions planned, resources, milestones, and completion dates. This type of action plan can be used by the coach to help the client articulate which development goals to choose and how to achieve them. The choice of goals is usually determined by feedback from assessments and other data collected by the coach. Chapter 4 explains the steps often followed in the coaching process.

Action Plan Format.   This form is an uncompleted action plan that you can reproduce and use in discussions with the coach and the client.

Sample Progress Report.   This resource provides an example of a brief report that the coach might use to discuss progress with the client as well as to keep you informed about the coaching engagement. It can be part of the Action Planning step discussed in Chapter 4.

"To-Do" List for Managing Coaching Resources.   If you have responsibility for managing coaching resources for your organization, this

list of actions and critical questions to ask yourself can be used so that you understand the purpose of the coaching and how it links to business strategy, and so that you can communicate it to others in the organization. See Chapter 5 for a more complete explanation of the actions required to manage the overall coaching program.

Common Coaching Situations

Those who are most likely to use coaching are people who are encountering a new and difficult challenge. These are some of the most common situations faced by men and women in today's organizations.

Coaching Clients	Things to Achieve	Considerations
Business Unit Heads	• Short-term financial results • Good relationship with Board • Growth in global markets • Merger and acquisition transitions	• Who should do the coaching? • How does one connect to business activities? • What are the criteria for an external coach? • Does the coach have credibility with the client?
High-Potential Talent	• Consistent high performance • Leveraging of strengths • Development of "challenge" areas • Developing organizational savvy	• Internal or external coach? • What is successful performance? • Does the individual learn new things quickly?

(Continued)

Executive Coaching. Copyright © 2005 by John Wiley & Sons, Inc. Reproduced by permission of Pfeiffer, an Imprint of Wiley. www.pfeiffer.com

Coaching Clients	Things to Achieve	Considerations
		• How tolerant is the organization to a long learning curve? • Will the organization tolerate some failures by the client?
Expatriates	• Understanding of new culture • Ability to achieve results in new culture • Interpersonal sensitivity to different customs • Managing amid possible chaos	• Does the coach possess understanding of how cultural differences show up? • How sensitive is the coach to multi-cultural issues? • How will the coach prioritize development plan actions that are affected most by cultural differences?
Women and Multi-Cultural Candidates	• Credibility as a leader • Leadership skills (communication, strategic planning, and so forth) • Networks within and outside the organization	• What characteristics of the coach will be most important to good chemistry? • How sensitive is the coach to diversity issues? • How much awareness does the coach possess about diversity within your organization's culture?
People on "Stretch" Assignments	• Demonstration of ability to achieve beyond previous levels • Short-term and possibly long-term business results • Excellence in execution	• How can I understand what constitutes high performance for the organization? • What new behaviors should be leveraged by the client?

Questions for an Interview
with a Prospective Coach

Here are some questions to add to your interview protocol when selecting the right coach. Elements of an appropriate response are provided in the bullet points.

1. Since the establishment of trust is so important to a coaching relationship, specifically what do you do in order to establish trust with a new client?

What to look for in a response:

- Appreciates the importance of trust

- Has a sense of what he or she needs to do to build a safe relationship

- Recognizes the need to establish a relationship with all stakeholders and knows how to proceed

2. Describe to me one of your most successful coaching engagements.

What to look for in a response:

- How was success measured?

- Who did what to make it succeed?

- Was credit shared?

3. Tell me about a time when you had a very challenging coaching assignment. What did you find most difficult about the assignment? What happened at the conclusion of the engagement?

What to look for in a response:

- Shared responsibility (cause and cure)

- How was the client's anger dealt with?

- How did the coach handle the pressure?

4. Describe what you would consider to be an unsuccessful coaching engagement. What did you learn from it? What would you do differently?

What to look for in a response:

- Were there learnings?

5. Describe the process you follow when you have a new client. What are the steps from the beginning to the middle and the end of the coaching engagement?

What to look for in a response:

- Is there a clear process?

- Is there flexibility in the process?

- Possible alternatives?

6. With what assessment instruments are you familiar? In what assessments are you certified?

What to look for in a response:

- How much does the coach rely primarily on assessments?

7. What other types of information do you like to obtain on a client?

What to look for in a response:

- Is there mention of observations in meetings, telephone calls, emails, and other written communications?

8. What do you include in an action plan?

What to look for in a response:

- How specific is it?

- What is the link to the business strategy?

- Are there long-term and short-term goals?

- How actionable are the items?

9. What are the company and industry experiences that will contribute to the success of this coaching assignment?

What to look for in a response:

- How relevant are the other experiences?

10. What do you do to ensure the confidentiality between you and the client?

What to look for in a response:

- Are clear expectations set with all stakeholders at the start of the engagement?

11. How do you provide progress reports to the HR professional and the client's supervisor?

What to look for in a response:

- How does progress track with goals?

- How frequently are reports made?

12. Under what circumstances will you refuse to take a case?

What to look for in a response:

- Client not motivated

- Client set up for failure

13. Under what circumstances will you halt an ongoing case?

What to look for in a response:

- Client not motivated

Agenda Items for an Initial Discussion Among HR Professional, Client, Boss, and Coach

Be sure there is clarity on the answers to the following questions, at a minimum, in your initial meeting with the client, boss, and coach.

- What is the overall business strategy for the business unit?

- What are the results required over the course of the next year for the business unit?

- How do the goals of the coaching assignment fit into the business strategy?

- In what ways can the client improve his or her own performance? The performance of the team? The performance of the business unit?

- How will success be measured?

- What information about the coaching assignment is to be shared? With whom? At what intervals?

- How often and to whom are progress reports given?

- What are the procedures for scheduling coaching sessions?

- What are the procedures for changing appointments? How are cancellations to be handled?

Sample Agreement for Coaching Services

This agreement describes the scope of work to be provided by [name of coach], [coach's organization], for executive coaching services for [Company X].

Project Objectives

The focus of the project is executive coaching with [name and title of client].

Coaching objectives for [name of client] include enabling her to do the following:

- Develop her leadership skills for current and future assignments in [Company X]

- Improve public speaking skills

- Develop specific leadership competencies in accordance with her competency survey feedback

- Broaden her repertoire of managerial styles

Components of the Coaching Program

The executive coaching program will consist of the following components:

- The creation of a comprehensive development action plan

- Direct observations of leadership behaviors with direct reports during team meetings

- Conducting interviews with selected employees

- Administration of appropriate assessment and survey instruments

- Scheduled, one-on-one coaching sessions with [name of client] that incorporate feedback from direct observations, interviews, and development plan objectives

Confidentiality

The coach-client discussions are confidential. Either the coach or the client will periodically provide a status report to [the supervisor, HR professional, or both] to confirm that the coaching continues on schedule and toward its objectives.

Time Frame and Fees

The executive coaching program will begin [month, day, year] and will be completed [month, day, year]. The program will require the equivalent of [X] days per month and the total rate for the project will be [$XXXXX]. [X] percentage of this total amount will be billed monthly for [X] months. Travel, room, and board, if incurred, will be billed at cost.

Agreement

By signing this agreement, both the coach and the client commit to the above provisions.

Coach-Consultant: _____   Date: _____

Client: _____   Date: _____

Client's supervisor (if appropriate):_____   Date: _____

Sample Action Plan

Goal

To improve the ability to provide visionary leadership to the business unit

Measures of Success

- Creation of communications on vision and mission

- Increases in revenue by X percent by year end

- Ability of employees to articulate the vision, mission, and their role in the success of the business unit

Action Steps	Resources Needed	Milestones	Completion Dates
Formulate vision, strategy, and objectives for business unit	• Overall corporate vision and goals • Analysis of industry trends • Strategy meetings with boss and peers • Input from direct reports	• Completion of strategy sessions • Creation of vision and strategy document	End of 1st quarter
Communication of vision and mission to business unit	• Prepare and give vision speech • Staff person assigned part-time to develop communication package	• Vision speech completed • Staff person assigned • Communication package completed	End of 2nd quarter
Track revenue increases	• Create relevant measures to track revenue increases • Create processes for direct reports to submit and use the data	• Measures created and agreed on by team • Revenue data is used to modify business unit strategy	End of 3rd quarter
Mission and vision are articulated by members of business unit	• Communication package • Vision speech	• Mission and vision are discussed in team meetings	End of 4th quarter

Action Plan Format

Goal:

Measures of Success:

Action Steps	Resources Needed	Milestones	Completion Dates

Sample Progress Report

Project Objectives

The focus of the project is executive coaching with [name and title of client]. Coaching objectives for [name of client] include enabling him/her to:

- Develop leadership skills for current and future assignments in [Company X]

- Develop specific leadership competencies in accordance with his/her competency survey feedback

- Broaden his/her repertoire of managerial styles

Progress to Date

The coaching objectives that have been targeted thus far have been to:

- Improve public speaking skills to large audiences of more than 300 people

Formulate and communicate the business strategy to
his/her organization

- Broaden his/her repertoire of managerial styles, particularly a coaching style that encourages the long-term development of direct reports

Milestones/Feedback on Public Speaking Skills

On [date], [client] delivered a presentation to 300 people in which he/she explained the vision and strategy for the organization. Feedback from peers and direct reports in the audience was highly favorable regarding the clarity of the message. Performance could have been improved by demonstrating greater ease and facility with the Q & A portion of the presentation

Feedback on Coaching Style

In the past two quarters, [client] has held quarterly one-on-one sessions with all direct reports for the purpose of discussing their professional long-term development goals.

Two staff members have received promotions, and one has moved laterally to broaden her skills.

Continuing coaching efforts will focus on development of other leadership competencies such as:

- Improving peer group teamwork

- Delegating responsibility clearly

The coaching is proceeding on schedule, and the client demonstrates motivation and a willingness to try out new skills and behaviors.

Coach: Date:

"To-Do" List for Managing Coaching Resources

Action	Questions to Ask Yourself
1. Clarify your strategy.	• What is the purpose of the coaching? • How does it link to the business strategy?
2. Connect coaching to other development efforts.	• How does the coaching reinforce lessons learned in training? • How can the coaching be used to enhance on-job experiences?
3. Develop a pool of coaches.	• What are the skills and abilities needed in a coach for your organization? For this client?
4. Be an effective gatekeeper.	• What are the criteria to determine whether coaching is needed or not?

Action	Questions to Ask Yourself
	• What other organization development efforts might occur simultaneously?
5. Monitor the PR.	• What can I do to help the organization realize the value of coaching as a methodology?
6. Support the executive as the primary client.	• How can I help the other stakeholders understand that the executive is the primary client?
7. Provide orientations to the organization.	• How can I help the coach understand the organization's strategic business plans and the role that the client plays in those plans?
	• What are the key informal relationships about which the coach needs to know in order for the coaching to be effective?

Appendix

· ·

This Appendix contains an Executive Breakaway Section, which is also posted on the Pfeiffer website (www.pfeiffer.com), intended to be used as informational reading for coaching clients. It may be photocopied or printed from the website and distributed to clients. It contains a summarized version of the key content of this book presented from the client's point of view.

Executive Breakaway Section

The purpose of this section is to provide you, the coaching client, with a better understanding of what to expect in a coaching relationship. It is written expressly to help you become a more savvy consumer of coaching services.

Topics covered in this section include the following:

- Why use a coach?

- How a coach can help

- How coaching starts

- Steps in the coaching process

- Electronic coaching

- Normal anxieties

- Ground rules and trust

- Taking responsibility

- The business relationship

- Time commitments

- Responsibilities to your boss and HR person

- Coachable moments

- Permission to speak up

Why Use a Coach?

You, the client, play the central role in the coaching story. We assume you've never been a coaching client before, so in this section we examine your role in helping to ensure the success of the coaching relationship.

Something in the way of a business challenge probably is causing the need for you to learn some new behaviors quickly. This challenge may appear as a change in the nature or scope of work, an assignment to turn around or fix a business, or a global or international assignment with a high level of complexity and ambiguity in it. Usually these challenges occur in clusters, possibly creating thoughts such as "It just never stops" or "I might be in over my head" or even "What am I supposed to do now?" Whatever it is, there is a need to ramp up quickly and accelerate the learning curve.

There are lots of ways to learn. Our early educational lives were typically dominated by "instruction" in one form or another. As we grow into adulthood, trial and error becomes perhaps the most common learning method. We also learn by reading about what others have done, watching what others do, or occasionally by going to formal classes. Personal coaching is also a learning alternative.

Coaching tends to be most appropriate when:

- Performance makes an important difference to the employer. Almost by definition, the contributions expected of senior executives fall into this category. Managers at other levels who are in especially significant roles also are responsible for making an important contribution, so they too can be appropriate coaching clients. Managers may receive coaching simply because they are considered to be "high potential," regardless of the nature of their current organizational role.

- The relevant learning issues are in the "soft skills" area. Improving any person's performance in these areas is often difficult and requires an intensive effort. Many of these coaching assignments fall into familiar categories:

  - Helping people with personal or self-management issues, such as a need to micromanage, time management difficulties, balancing work and family life, or perhaps a career-related concern

  - Helping people who have assertive, dominant, or controlling styles become better able to build relationships, create trust, delegate, work in teams, or develop their subordinates

  - Helping people who have good "people" skills to be better at calling the tough decisions, setting and enforcing standards, and handling conflict in productive ways

  - Helping people develop leadership skills when they have moved (or are about to move) into a more prominent role (Some typical leadership issues are providing vision and strategy, performing symbolic roles, and functioning in a much more "alone" position without getting much valid feedback.)

- Used in conjunction with formal succession planning programs.

- Associated with executive development programs. Lessons learned offsite may be combined with on-the-job assignments and the support of a coach when the formal program is over.

- There are no right answers, you need to develop your own solutions to certain of the puzzles of executive life, and it's hard to do it on your own. If there were right answers hidden away somewhere, the task would be a lot easier.

- The learning needs to happen according to your schedule, and quickly. People who are moved into important positions with little advance notice can be supported with a coach.

- Assimilating new hires, or another term for this is "on-boarding."

The common theme throughout this list is the need to deal with a steep learning curve.

How a Coach Can Help

What actually happens in the coaching relationship that allows you to get better at interpersonal skills, communicating, delegating, time management, emotional self-management, or other soft skills? How does someone focus on and improve these kinds of skills?

First, let's agree that these skills are not of the kind that can be learned in a classroom setting. Rather, they are learned by direct interaction with others while working. Sometimes this is called "action learning." This is the way adults learn best, and this is the model that best applies to interpersonal skills. With the coach's help, a feedback loop is created based on trying out new behaviors, followed by feedback and reflection, and then trying again to be as effective at whatever is happening.

Here are some of the things the coach and the coaching process contribute to the learning:

- *Focus of attention.* Having a coach means paying attention to the issues. Appointments are scheduled, time is spent, and discussions are held regarding the relevant topics.

- *Self-discipline.* Because of the regularity of appointments and the involvement of other people, it's a lot easier to stay on track. Organizational life is full of distractions, even emergencies. Having a coach is a way to increase the priority of this change effort.

- *Valid data.* Change and learning require good data, and the coach can help bring that about. Information is needed on what you bring to the job, what actions are effective, and what is needed in order to succeed. A coach may offer his or her personal views of your actions and/or may do some "testing" using standardized inventories. The coach can interview others in the organization to get their views confidentially. The coach can help interpret 360-degree surveys, attitude surveys, or performance reviews. Perhaps most importantly, the coach can help you make sense of all this data.

- *New ideas.* The coach may or may not have held a job such as yours. But he or she has worked with a lot of people like you and knows something about how they have succeeded. The coach brings new perspective to your thinking and helps you get out of mental ruts and dead ends. Not all the ideas are brilliant—or will work for you. Nonetheless, there's a pool of suggestions waiting for you to check out.

- *Support*. It's not easy to do things differently. In addition to your own ingrained habits, your colleagues may have you fixed in their minds as a person who does things in a certain way. Making changes means taking risks, persevering in the face of resistance, and possibly feeling a little strange or silly at times. Changes require a "safe" environment in which to takes these risks. The coach is there to provide encouragement, help, and someone to talk to while all this is happening.

- *The learning process*. Sometimes the greatest value coming out of a coaching relationship isn't just your changed behavior or the changed perceptions of others in the organization. Sometimes it is your insight into *how* to learn. The coach's expertise is exactly in this domain, and some of it should rub off on you over the course of your relationship.

A coaching assignment is triggered by an opportunity or a glitch or a transition of one kind or another. There will be many more opportunities, glitches, and transitions in life, but a coach won't be there for most of them. If you take away good insights into *how* to handle the learning/change process, and a sense as to how to use these insights in future situations, then you will be the real winner.

How Coaching Starts

Coaching puts you in a very *active* role. This is a shift from the role you played when you were a student or a patient seeking help from a doctor. Nothing much of importance will happen as a result of coaching unless you try to make it happen. All the other participants in the story are supporting characters—it is really all about you and what you want to do.

This active role begins at the very beginning, when the first discussion is held about coaching. You should make an active decision to be a coaching client. Perhaps you initiated the idea. If someone approached you about it, your participation should be voluntary. Ideally, you should enter this relationship with positive energy and curiosity. Unbridled enthusiasm is too much to expect from a first-time participant, but you certainly shouldn't be coerced into this activity.

You should be comfortable about doing the coaching at this time. By "this time" we mean that the flow of your work suggests that coaching might be helpful now and that you're comfortable with your boss and HR professional as participants. This is also a decision on your part.

Similarly, you may have been actively involved with the choice of who your coach will be and what the two of you will focus on.

So now it's time to actually start the coaching relationship. What should you be doing to make it worthwhile? What are you likely to be experiencing during the coaching?

Steps in the Coaching Process

Coaching relationships are custom-designed, not replicated from a manual the coach keeps on a shelf or that the HR department asks external coaches to obey. However, a large percentage of coaching assignments do follow a general format, which is what we will describe here. If you feel your situation falls outside of the usual pattern for coaching assignments, you will need to contract for a variation on the traditional relationship so you will have a process that makes sense for you and your company.

Steps in the coaching process usually are delineated at the out-set of a coaching engagement. Although the names and labels may vary, in almost all situations a coaching process will contain these steps:

1. Contracting

2. Initial goal setting

3. Assessment

4. Implementation and action planning

5. Evaluation

1. Contracting

Coaching is possible only when there is mutual agreement. Regard-less of whether there is a formal, written contract, there has to be an initial step in which a general understanding is reached among you, the HR professional, your boss, and the coach about what's going to happen. Your HR professional may wish to set up an ini-tial meeting with all parties to discuss the issues.

Usually the agreement is more formal with the HR profes-sional and the organization and less formal with you. A continuum of formality is possible, ranging from a one-paragraph email to a formal contract with a non-disclosure agreement.

The purpose here is not to create rigidity or arbitrary limitations. Rather, a clearly understood coaching process is important because predictability builds trust. A good structure also allows for discus-sion of variations to the plan, as needed.

Perhaps the most important element in the success of a coach-ing engagement is the bond or "chemistry" between you and the coach. A lot has been written, but very little decided, on what goes into the magic of a good bond. During the contracting step there has to be a sense from both parties that "This is going to work" or "I trust this person." Of course, the relationship can be terminated at any time later on, but there have to be positive feelings at the outset—or there is no contract!

A contract, memo, or letter of agreement will typically address the following points:

- How often you and your coach will meet and for approximately how long, for example, two or three times each month for about an hour

- A starting and possible ending date

- The general focus of the coaching, such as project leadership skills, an abrasive interpersonal style, time management, or work/family balance issues

- Some sense of how "success" will be measured—how the wrap-up and evaluation might proceed

- Reporting and confidentiality—who can say what to whom

- Costs (if the letter is going to the person who pays the bills)

When asked about which steps are most valuable to the coaching process, one HR professional from a large technology company replied: "The contracting phase is critical to do with the client and the client's supervisor so that there are appropriate expectations set by everyone involved. All of the parties involved, the client, the boss, the HR person and the coach, must understand the goals and objectives of the coaching. It also helps to convey to the coach the possible future plans for the client and what is contained in a succession plan if one actually does exist for that individual. At that point, it is incumbent on the coach to develop a coaching plan to help the client achieve the desired goals."

Information Sharing

One of the main requirements in coaching is trust. Any successful coaching relationship is built on mutual trust between the coach and the client. The relationship is based on privileged communication between you and your coach, and often the information that is exchanged may be potentially damaging. If there is a breakdown in trust, the coaching engagement is clearly bound to fail. Therefore, the issue of confidentiality is crucial to coaching.

When being coached, you will share delicate private and corporate information with your coach in order to explore developmental opportunities. Naturally, this situation may cause concerns from your perspective as well as from the coach's perspective. You might wonder who else has access to the information. How can you be assured that the information is not shared with someone you don't trust? Who knows that you are being coached? Will the information shared have an impact on your promotion or salary?

The coach, who is usually paid by your organization, faces a different conflict: Am I obliged to share a progress report with my client's supervisor, Human Resources, or the sponsor? If so, how much detail do I go into? Who in the organization needs to be informed if my client shares information about illegal wrongdoings involving either the client or other organizational members? All these concerns are legitimate and need to be addressed before attempting to build a trusting, open relationship.

If you believe that your coach is sharing private information or if the coach feels caught up in an organizational power struggle, the relationship is likely to crumble. Confidentiality is therefore both an ethical and a practical issue.

Ethical Standards

Whereas doctors, lawyers, priests, and others whose professions require dealing with personal information are bound by the law to apply certain ethical standards, there are no explicit laws in that regard applicable for coaches. For those coaches who are psychologists, the ethical standards concerning disclosures in the profession of psychology apply. Although the coach has to try to make every effort to honor your confidence, the coach cannot provide a guarantee. You should be aware that your information is not privileged under law.

Best Practice

In order to avoid conflicts, the coach is well advised to discuss the issue of confidentiality up-front with you. By making you aware that there are usually other stakeholders in the coaching process, such as your supervisor, the HR manager, or others, your coach can discuss with you which information is shared and which information is kept confidential. Ideally, during the contracting phase, a meeting between you, your coach, your boss, and the HR professional has occurred in which issues of confidentiality have been discussed. Who does the reporting? How much write-up is needed? It makes sense to share information about goals and progress, but not the contents of coach-client discussions.

The other possibility is to encourage you to inform other stakeholders about your developmental process. This can either be done in the presence of the coach or in private. In any case, you and your coach must reach a joint agreement that leaves you both in your comfort zones and sets a solid basis for a trusting relationship. By reaching an agreement about confidentiality in the first place, most conflicts of interest can be avoided.

2. Initial Goal Setting

A first draft of goals—What is to be accomplished by the coaching?—should be part of the contracting step. It may look like a simple thing to do, but it is not.

- Client, coach, HR professional, and boss all may wish to see somewhat different outcomes. These expectations must be articulated and conflicts explored and resolved.

- As the coaching process evolves, what is considered to be a realistic and desired goal may change.

- There may be interim goals as well as long-term goals.

- There may be "business" and also "personal" goals—and they may overlap and impact each other.

A reasonable approach, therefore, is to set an initial goal and expect to confirm or revise it as time goes by.

Goal setting is central to the process. Well-defined goals allow you to work together, to assess progress and success, to choose appropriate methods and relevant data, and so on. Good coaching is results-oriented and does not wander off into unimportant tangents. It is important for the coach to understand the business challenges facing both you and the organization.

The goal for many coaching engagements is expressed in behavioral terms. For example, you will do more or less of something, or learn to do something, or stop doing something. Some typical goals in executive coaching address improvement in leadership competencies, specific interpersonal and social competencies, and the ability to manage your career issues. Other goals may explicitly

and implicitly involve increasing the effectiveness of the organization and team.

When possible, it will be useful to define the coaching goal in
"business" terms—connecting it to operating plans or financial measures. This is often not possible, however desirable it might be. It is
generally sufficient for the goal to be agreed on by the four interested parties—you, your coach, HR, and your boss. Both your needs
and the employer's interests must be served. This agreement may be
easy to reach or may be negotiated.

3. Assessment

Good coaching rests on a foundation of good data. It is important
for the coach to quickly ascertain your performance level in order
to understand the magnitude of the gap between current performance and future desired performance. Questions your coach will
have include: How are you currently functioning? What has to
improve or change for you to maximize performance? The coach
has to determine the overall pattern of strengths and challenge areas
to help you set goals for improvements in job performance. You and
your coach must be able to operate together with a common language and set of concepts. The most efficient way for the coach to
go about this is by systematically collecting data on those behavioral dimensions that have the most impact on performance. Why
collect data? As an executive, you are comfortable looking at data.
Multiple perspectives create a richer picture. Coaching shouldn't
be based on hunches; objective data is of value. Data gathering
can be done in lots of ways. Some alternatives for gathering information are described below:

- *Interviews.* The coach will create an interview protocol
  and conduct either individual face-to-face or telephone

interviews. Interviews can be conducted with direct reports, peers, supervisors, and others in the organization who have a high degree of familiarity with you. The results from the interviews are summarized separately and reviewed with you, along with the data from other sources.

- *Multi-rater feedback assessments.* Sometimes these are also called 360-degree feedback instruments. In addition to making "self" ratings, usually you are asked to provide a list of raters from the following categories: direct reports, peers, current and past supervisors, and customers. Most multi-rater feedback tools are now available so that the entire administration is done electronically. Typically, once you have provided the raters' email addresses to the survey administrator, the raters receive a web address and a password. When the raters access the website and type in a preassigned password, they can take the surveys at their convenience. Reports may be generated electronically and emailed to the coach, who delivers the feedback to you.

- *Testing.* Some coaches use individual psychometric tests. Some tests require professional qualifications, either through a certification process by the publisher or by educational background. In the hands of a competent practitioner, they can be very helpful. These include personality tests, interest inventories, learning styles, and interpersonal style tests.

- *Existing qualitative and quantitative data from performance appraisals, attitude surveys, customer satisfaction surveys, and training programs.* The information from these sources can be very helpful to the coach, particularly at the start of a coaching program, because it provides insight into how you, the client, are being perceived by various parts of the organization.

- *Observations of you, the client.* Experienced coaches have skills in observing and recording behavior, and the information gathered from direct observations of you during meetings, phone calls, and presentations can be very useful. The coach may also ask to see written materials from you such as emails. All of this can provide powerful real-world data, especially when combined with data from assessments.

How much historical data to include? This depends on the nature of your issues. It can be really helpful for the coach to understand client behaviors that may have a long history. And it can be helpful for you to reflect back and gain greater self-awareness and insight. However, the focus of the coaching should be on how the behavior will become more adaptive in the present and future.

What You Should Know About Multi-Rater Feedback

Multi-rater feedback can be used to support coaching, either to help a client develop his or her potential or to address a performance concern. Such data can be useful for identifying development needs of future leaders. It is helpful for communicating behaviors consistent with new organizational values or principles or to provide senior leaders with valid data so they can make fine-tuned adjustments to their leadership styles. Typically, results are shared only with a client, who now "owns" the data.

Here are several important points that should make using such surveys a success, especially in combination with coaching:

- It is a good idea for you to identify most or maybe even all of the raters. Chances are that you will be reasonable about whom you choose. It is important that you not "stack the deck" by including only raters who have a highly favorable opinion of you! By selecting a broad variety of raters, you are likely to get far more credible data. And you will receive some very valuable information about how you are perceived by others.

- If you have questions about the process, ask! Take the time to have your HR professional explain to you and to the raters what the survey is, what it does, how it is used, and its benefits to all concerned.

- Even if a professional coach facilitates the feedback, it is important for your manager and HR representative to be familiar with the rating instrument and how it is used.

Need for Reflection Following Feedback

Once the data have been integrated and summarized, the coach will feed back the information to you, usually over more than one session. Because there is usually much information to reflect on, it is better if you absorb only some at a time. Sometimes you will be surprised by certain aspects of the data and you will need time to reflect and think it all through.

During the course of your coaching engagement, you can expect to be doing more self-reflection. This may seem uncomfortable for you at first. However, if you can learn to incorporate time for reflection into your schedule, you will benefit greatly. Coaching can accelerate the learning process, and by making the time to think through your issues, you are allowing valuable learning to take place.

After the data from assessments and other sources has been reviewed, it makes sense to go back to the goals that were created earlier to see whether any new ones need to be added and to reprioritize those that have been retained.

4. Implementation and Action Planning

The coaching process can move into an implementation and action-planning phase when:

- The initial goal of the coaching has been determined

- The coaching agreement has set expectations for how the coaching engagement will proceed

- The coach has had the opportunity to become familiar with different aspects of your behavior from the assessment results

In helping you explore and learn new concepts and skills, coaches may employ a variety of coaching methods and techniques. Which methods a coach may choose will depend on the background and training of the coach, the unique interaction between you and your coach, and the coach's views on which approaches would be most effective within a given organization. Fundamentally, a coaching process allows you to take the time to reflect on and explore issues that affect your and the organization's effectiveness. Although every interaction between a coach and a client is unique, some of the common elements that could occur during implementation are

- *Exploring for alternatives*. You benefit from gaining greater self-knowledge by understanding your feedback data, reviewing previously successful and unsuccessful efforts at behavior change, gathering new ideas, reading, and observing others. In your sessions, the coach frequently poses questions to encourage you to engage in reflective thought. The coach provides a supportive relationship in which you are stimulated to explore new ideas, feelings, and behaviors. Often, the role of the coach is described as that of a catalyst.

- *Experimenting with new behaviors*. The trust that is established between you and your coach enables you to experiment with new behaviors that may feel very foreign initially, but which, in the long run, add to your repertoire of adaptable responses. Some of the techniques that help clients to feel more comfortable and competent as they adopt new ways of interacting with others are

  - *Rehearsing or role playing*. Being able to practice possible responses to anticipated situations lets you polish skills and reduce some of the anxiety associated with the fear of the unknown.

  - *Visioning*. Professional athletes have known for quite a while that increments in performance can be realized just by imagining oneself giving a peak performance. Whether it is a competency such as speaking to a large audience or maintaining one's composure during meetings, if you can practice visioning optimal performance, you are partway there.

- *Problem solving.* Coaches generally are good at asking
  clients questions to stimulate their thinking to arrive
  at creative solutions. The idea is that eventually you
  may learn to do creative problem solving on your own.

- *Role clarification.* Understanding everyone's role in a
  given business/social situation can help you to act
  appropriately and pick up important social cues. A
  coach can help you foster role clarity for yourself
  within your organization.

- *Creating an action plan.* An action plan consists of several components. It can be used to establish a goal,
  define the measures that will be used to determine
  whether the goal has been reached, explain the actions
  to be taken to reach the goal, the resources needed, significant milestones, and completion dates. This type of
  action plan can be used by you and your coach in
  tracking development goals.

- *Gathering support and getting feedback from colleagues.*
  The chances of a successful coaching outcome are
  enhanced when you can be open with your colleagues
  about the desired changes. Enlisting their commitment
  increases the likelihood that you will receive accurate
  feedback as new behaviors are explored and practiced.

- *Devising a long-term development plan.* This may be
  optional for you and focuses on personal goals over a
  longer timeframe. Sometimes you can use it for career
  management and to advance professionally. A long-
  term development plan can serve as preparation
  for future roles and contributions. It can also help
  you avoid backsliding once the coaching assignment
  is over.

5. Evaluation

There are many good reasons to evaluate the results of a coaching assignment. First, the organization will want to know whether your performance is improving or not. Have you succeeded in making the behavioral changes needed to improve leadership? To stay informed about progress on goals, your HR professional may want to receive occasional reports from the coach.

Second, the HR professional will want to determine the impact of the coaching on others in the organization. Has the allocation of resources yielded results for both you and the organization? How do others perceive the changes that are occurring?

Third, the evaluation serves as a recalibration process. It can provide valuable information for you and your coach that helps you make adjustments in the coaching. Which new behaviors are being demonstrated and which ones are not? How does the focus of the coaching need to shift? What job experiences do you need at this juncture? What feedback should the boss provide to you at this point in time?

Fourth, the outcome of the evaluation can serve as powerful reinforcement for the work effort involved in coaching. What successes can you and your coach celebrate? Where are renewed efforts required? What should be the content of the boss's communications to you in order to provide both reinforcement and incentive?

Finally, the evaluation can show where the action plan requires updating and revision. Are the coaching goals still appropriate or do they need rethinking?

A good time to specify the details of an evaluation of the coaching program is at the contracting phase. An evaluation process can help in establishing clarity at the outset about what the coaching is designed to accomplish. The memo or letter of agreement can address the topic of how success will be measured.

When it comes to a formal evaluation, a number of approaches are possible. The methods used for gathering information during the assessment phase can be used as measurements of performance between the initial data collection (Time 1) and a later point (Time 2). It's a good idea to allow at least six months between Time 1 and Time 2 to allow you the opportunity to develop new behaviors. It also takes time for others in the organization to notice your new behavior patterns! One or two demonstrations may not be convincing evidence for others to accept that you are truly doing things differently.

Evaluations can be based on any of the following sources of data:

- *Interviews*. If interviews were done at the start of the coaching engagement, it may be appropriate for the coach to reassess or reinterview the same respondents and compare responses from Time 1 to Time 2. How do the interview themes between Time 1 and Time 2 differ? Are you demonstrating more adaptive behaviors and fewer disruptive ones?

- *Multi-rater feedback assessments*. With this form of feedback, it is especially important to wait at least six months before a reevaluation and to recognize that it is a pattern of changes that will be significant.

- *Informal feedback from others*. On a more informal basis, the boss and selected individuals may be asked how you are doing. This information can be written in a progress report that is completed by the coach or jointly by you and your coach. With the exception of the input provided by the boss, it is a good idea for the feedback to be aggregated so that statements cannot be attributed to one person alone. Protecting the anonymity of raters ensures that the feedback will be more accurate and reduces raters' fear of reprisal.

- *Performance appraisals, attitude surveys, customer satisfaction surveys, and training program surveys.* Since many of these measures are administered infrequently, they may or may not coincide with the evaluation period of the coaching program. Also, the actual questions on surveys often change from year to year so that the measure from Time 1 to Time 2 may not be consistent. With the possible exception of the performance appraisal, these instruments may not be sensitive enough to pick up the kinds of behaviors that you are attempting to change. However, taking all of this into account, the coach may still want to see the results from these sources of data, especially if at least a year has elapsed from the time of both the first measurement and the start of the coaching program.

- *Client feedback.* Are you satisfied? Feedback from you may be given directly to the coach, or to the HR professional, the boss, and others in the organization. If periodic progress reports are written jointly by you and your coach, you may have the opportunity to provide more formal feedback. Often, however, you may simply tell your HR professional how valuable the coaching has been in accelerating the required new learning.

- *Action plans.* The coaching may have involved the creation of an action plan that defines goals, measures of success, and completion dates. Was the action plan created and implemented successfully? Were useful goals set? Were the goals achieved? Is there a business outcome? A behavioral change? How did the organization benefit from the action plans?

- *Long-term development plans.* Sometimes coaching leads to a long-term personal development plan. Was this prepared, and is there agreement to do something about it?

Finally, a good contracting process will provide some sense of how the coaching program will be wrapped up. You will want to keep your HR professional informed about that final phase of the coaching process. Did you and your coach openly discuss what has and has not been achieved?

Sometimes, there is a clear ending after a relatively intense process. More frequently, the coaching is continued with less-frequent sessions or on an as-needed basis and becomes more of an informal relationship with some level of paid involvement. There may also be a "planned follow-up" after a specified period of time. Usually, some closure is needed on the more formal, intense phase of the coaching.

Electronic Coaching

In the future, coaches are likely to do more coaching via the telephone and the Internet. There are several reasons for this trend:

- *Globalization.* Organizational functions will continue to become more global in nature. Your coaching sessions may not be able to be scheduled when both you and your coach are in the same geographical location.

- *Cost-effectiveness.* It can be more cost-effective for coaches to deliver services electronically.

- *Technological improvements*. The improvements in voice quality in cell phones, computers with video, and other technological devices have increased the level of comfort in conducting long-distance conversations about personal/career issues.

Many coaches will use emails as a way of following up on points made during a session or will send information on topics related to your goals for your use between sessions. Emails can be very effective in fostering your ability for self-reflection. They require that senders be more thoughtful in their choice of words and allow readers more time to review and think carefully about the contents.

Whether or not emails are utilized more in the coaching process, the steps in the coaching process should remain the same. Usually the initial contracting and goal setting can still occur via several face-to-face meetings in which you and the coach have the opportunity to forge the chemistry essential to a good coaching relationship. The ability of the coach to see facial expressions and body language is important for the coach to get to know you. It also allows the coach to create a visual picture of you, to more accurately interpret your communications, and to see exactly what others also see when they engage with you.

Normal Anxieties

At the very onset of a coaching engagement, it is normal to feel a bit anxious and vulnerable. You are starting on a high-disclosure, high-vulnerability adventure with a stranger. There's only so much comfort you can gain from an initial chemistry-check meeting. The contracting sessions should help you get started by reaching mutual agreement about goals and confidentiality. Still, there may be a lingering sense of uncertainty as you embark on an unknown journey. For the coaching to have a successful outcome resulting in change and personal growth, it is wise to recognize that these feelings may accompany you at the outset.

What might you be anxious about? One answer to this question is that *all* changes come with some amount of stress. This is true for weddings, benchmark birthdays, promotions and new jobs, the birth of children, relocations—all the transitions and milestones of living, even the most joyous of them. Unhappy events certainly bring out a number of unsettling emotions. Coaching is associated with some degree of change in your public leadership style, and that too can be a transition. The outcome may be only a fine-tuning or a minor adjustment, but it may lead to something more substantial as well.

Another source of anxiety has to do with what happens if the coaching turns out *not* to be successful. Was it your fault? Does it mean you've reached a dead end in your career? Are you derailed or plateaued? Has your fatal flaw been discovered? In almost all cases, these are just anxieties and not likely to be realities. Coaching is not a surefire solution to problems, nor is it guaranteed to make the most of an opportunity. Many executives use a number of coaches over the course of their careers. It's not uncommon for a client to have some anxiety. These anxieties can be discussed with the coach, of course, or with the boss or HR representative. Our experience suggests that these concerns quickly fade away in most cases.

A comment is useful here regarding human "flaws." A much better word might be limitations, sore spots, things we're not proud of, even our secrets. Coaching does go better when there is a free exchange about motivations and personal histories. You are perfectly within your rights, however, to draw limits. For example, you might mention that you had a messy divorce, a troubled childhood, a severe medical problem, or a traumatic military experience. There's no obvious need to go further than that. If that history isn't relevant to your current or future position in the organization, then either don't deal with it or deal with it elsewhere.

Sometimes people are anxious about letting go of habits or styles they've owned for many years. You might be feeling something like "I wouldn't be me if I didn't do things that way" or "I really don't want to stop being an analytic, detailed kind of person." Coaches are aware that some aspects of our characters are very deeply ingrained. Coaching isn't about deep character reconstructions. It's more likely to be about managing how this character shows up at work. If you find a behavior that is not helping, then you'll consider ways to control, modify, or redirect it. You'll still be the same person, but with more effective behaviors.

Ground Rules and Trust

One of a coach's first tasks is to create "safety" in the relationship. It is his or her job to make that happen, but you can help too.

The structure of the coaching engagement serves as a roadmap for your interactions with your coach. By following the steps in the coaching process, as described earlier or as agreed on between the two of you, you have a framework with a beginning, a middle, and an end. The framework allows you to set expectations appropriately, recognize milestones and time limits, and celebrate your successes. A planned journey along a well-lit path allows for more trust and cooperation. Discussions with your coach about the ground rules will take much of the mystery out of the journey and help you to understand how you can help make the relationship work well.

It is wise to ease whatever concerns you might have by asking your coach the questions that are on your mind. There is no such thing as a dumb, honest question. All first-timers have questions, whatever it is they are doing. Often some of the early inquiries "get the ball rolling" and lead right into important areas for further discussion. By asking your questions without letting them simmer, you will feel more comfortable and build trust with your coach. Trust between people is built slowly over a series of many interactions, so your early experiences with your coach are critical for establishing a strong relationship. You will want to feel reassured that your coach "has what it takes" to guide you through the journey of self-exploration and personal development.

Coaching engagements evolve over time. There's no way to know exactly how things will progress or whether revisions will be needed in the ground rules, the goals, or the methods. Feel free to talk about these with your coach.

Taking Responsibility

You owe it to yourself to take responsibility for the coaching-related changes. After all, it's your life! You should be the "owner" of the goals for the coaching and for the steps for achieving them. When these are reasonably clear in your mind, then move forward boldly. Accept feedback from whatever sources—assessment instruments, official appraisals, informal comments, your coach's interviews—and make good use of it. Try new ways of doing things. Get feedback from people who saw you do things differently. Learn what helps and what doesn't. Your coach can serve as a catalyst, but ultimately it is only you who can make change happen.

Coaching requires that you give voice to your thoughts, hopes, and feelings. If this is not something you normally do, then at first you may feel as if you are exercising an unused muscle. Allow yourself to work through this and keep going. It comes more easily when you accept the ownership and responsibility for making a success of the coaching effort. The coach can only be a catalyst—you have to make it happen.

This is obvious, but not easy. Why is it difficult? For the same kinds of reasons that diets, good health habits, and New Year's resolutions are difficult. Just because it makes sense doesn't mean we'll do things that way. We're accustomed to putting blame on other people, procrastinating, expecting others to change first, even being lazy. Recall the corny old joke that goes "How many people does it take to change a light bulb? Only one, but the bulb really has to want to change." It's really not so funny when we think about all the good intentions we've had that went nowhere, and not for good reasons at all.

So what can you do to overcome this tendency? A few hints: Go public with your planned changes—it makes it harder to backslide. Enlist the support of others; ask for their active support. Keep a log or diary of efforts and successes. Reward yourself when things go according to plan.

The Business Relationship

The relationship between you and your coach is a business relationship: you and/or your organization purchases professional services from the coach to help both you and the sponsoring organization. There are likely to be both short- and long-term business benefits.

The outcome of the coaching benefits many others beyond the individual who receives the coaching, including direct reports, peers, supervisors, and anyone else who may be affected by a strengthening of leadership in one part of the organization. A ripple effect of good things can be created when the changes in behavior of one individual are perceived by others in the organization.

This is especially true if it is the leadership of a boss or a peer that is strengthened. Improvements in the morale of a group can occur. Individuals may be inspired to start on their own agendas for personal growth. The "return on investment" from successful coaching has the potential to be quite large.

With this in mind, you should know how the business relationship will be defined and how value will be assessed. It will help you frame your questions and form your answers if you approach the endeavor as you would approach any business project. To the extent possible, there will be a clear set of goals and objectives, action plans with milestones, and a means of evaluating the outcome.

Time Commitments

You and your coach will arrive at an understanding of the time commitments associated with the coaching. This will have been done in the contracting process as well as in your discussion on ground rules. Having a schedule and keeping to it are important aspects of the structure of the relationship. They also are good predictors of a successful outcome. In today's business environment, it is very easy to allow other events and meetings to crowd out your coaching time. It is common for urgent things to take priority over important things.

Making changes in your leadership or interpersonal style is the kind of task that requires continuity. That's why regular contact with the coach is important. Making these changes can be difficult, lonely work. Sticking to the schedule is a shared responsibility of both you and your coach, but slippage is much more often due to pressures on the client than on the coach.

Do your best to take responsibility for maintaining the integrity of the coaching schedule, just as you would for any other business obligation. Sometimes the coach serves as a kind of conscience, reminding you to stick to the process. However, your coach shouldn't have to become a nag!

If you do find that time commitments cannot be kept, have an open discussion with your coach. Maybe now isn't a good time. Maybe something is not working well in the relationship and the schedule slippage is a symptom of a larger problem.

Responsibilities to Your Boss and HR Person

The organization has invested its resources in you. Your boss and your HR person have agreed that your professional growth is important enough that time and money can be set aside for your development. What is your responsibility to them? What should be the nature and frequency of the feedback to them? Who should do it? The answer to these questions varies depending on your level in the organization and on your relationships with these people. There are no solid rules about this, but there are some good rules of thumb.

Your organization has a vested interest in hearing about your progress directly from you. At the very least you will want to give periodic updates to your boss and HR person on how the coaching is proceeding.

They will want to know whether the relationship is working well, whether they should be doing something to help it along, and whether their observations could be helpful. They are busy people too and aren't thinking about you and your coach every day. They also don't want to intrude into your private conversations. So it's helpful if you'd remember to keep them posted once in a while, even if things are going well. You may want to obtain a sense of their expectations concerning how often and in what modality they would like to be updated (voice, face-to-face, or email). If things aren't going well, then of course you should speak up.

It is generally better for you to keep the boss and the HR person up-to-date, rather than having the coach do it all. The coach's opinions are valued, of course, but what they really want to see is progress and growth in you! In any case, you don't want the coach to do all that work alone.

There may also be some differences in the extent to which you communicate your progress to them depending on your level in the organization. More senior-level executives are less likely to keep the HR person and the boss up-to-date. They also may request that the coach keep conversations with others to a minimum. Although this may be more comfortable for you, it doesn't necessarily serve your best interests. Those at middle or first-level manager levels typically have less ability to operate with this kind of independence.

Coachable Moments

Some of the most valuable learning experiences come from "coachable moments." These are the occasions when you recognize that something important is happening that has to do with the focus of your coaching. If you want the coach's help, speak up! Any coach will make time for you. If you need only a few minutes, or if a crisis is happening and you need more time, that's what coaches are for.

What do coachable moments look like? Crises are one example, but there are many others as well. It could be a situation that causes a peak in your anxiety level—a sense that trouble is lurking. It could be an insight, an epiphany of some kind that says, "Now I get it!" It could be some negative feedback. It could be that an opportunity has come up to try out a new way of doing things.

The following is an example of a coachable moment:

Don had been working with his coach, Sheila, for about two months. The coaching focused on two goals:

1. Helping Don move effectively into a "manager of managers" role, a task that resulted from his promotion just before the coaching started, and

2. Building a constructive—and he hoped cooperative—relationship with Helen, one of his new peers.

Sheila and Don had moved through the phases of contracting, assessment, and goal setting and had settled into a rhythm of meetings every two weeks or so. Progress was being made on the first goal with his four direct reports—new boundaries were established, he had moved his own style away from micromanaging to allow them a very significant degree of autonomy, a revised follow-up system was in place, and informal relationships were improving.

But Helen remained aloof. She and Don were cordial to each other, but no real connection was being made. Don wasn't sure whether Helen resented him for some past misstep or just didn't trust him yet. Other hypotheses were discussed in the coaching sessions, most recently on a Monday. Sheila and Don even sketched out possible scenarios for how Don could try to engage Helen in the areas where their work overlapped. Don was prepared to approach Helen with one of these conversations after the upcoming departmental meeting on Thursday.

On Tuesday of that week, about 10:00 a.m., Don called Sheila with a sense of urgency. He had received a call from Helen at 9:30 a.m. asking for a meeting that day. When he asked Helen what she wanted to talk about, her answer had to do with a need to borrow some of his key people for a few days to finish a major client assignment before the end of the week. Don and Helen agreed to meet at 2:00 p.m. that day. Don was looking for help from his coach on how to handle Helen's request.

Don wasn't sure what to do. Should he ask his boss? Should he ask for volunteers? Should he just tell his people to drop whatever they were doing so they could help Helen? He knew his people were stretched to do their own work. He didn't like any of the alternatives.

Sheila recognized this as a coachable moment. Sheila cleared her schedule so she could give Don the time he needed, which turned out to be more than an hour.

By noon, Don was clear about what he should do. He called a meeting of his direct reports. They developed a solution so that workloads were shared across organizational lines, priorities were maintained, and Helen got the help she needed. His 2:00 p.m. meeting with Helen, which included two of his direct reports, went smoothly. His relationships with his own people were honored and strengthened, and he built a bridge to Helen.

You will, no doubt, have many coachable moments in the course of your coaching engagement. Discussions with your coach can be helpful in helping you figure out which moments would be most beneficial to bring to the attention of your coach.

Permission to Speak Up

It should be clear by now that you own the coaching relationship. Although the organization has invested its resources in you and you have the support of other key individuals, the outcome of the coaching engagement is in your hands. At any and all times you have permission to speak up about your ideas. And why not? You will have permission from your coach. You will have permission from the organization. You just need to make sure that you have permission from yourself!

Conclusion

This section was written with the purpose of taking some of the mystery out of the coaching process. We hope it has enabled you to have a clearer picture of what happens as you begin your journey with your coach and make progress during your coaching relationship. You may also wish to go to your HR professional with other questions you might have regarding your particular situation and how the coaching process will work for you within your organization.

Bibliography

. . . .

Coaching Issues and Techniques

Bracken, D.W., Timmreck, C.W., & Church, A.H. (2001). *The handbook of multi-source feedback*. San Francisco, CA: Jossey-Bass.

Ciampa, D., & Watkins, M. (1999). *Right from the start*. Boston, MA: Harvard Business School Press.

Dotlich, D.L., & Cairo, P.C. (2003). *Why CEO's fail: The 11 behaviors that can derail your climb to the top and how to manage them*. San Francisco, CA: Jossey-Bass.

Downey, D., March, T., & Berkman, A. (2001). *Assimilating new leaders*. New York: AMACOM.

Edwards, M.R., & Ewen, A.J. (1996). *360-degree feedback: The powerful new model for employee assessment and performance improvement*. New York: American Management Association.

Frisch, M.H. (2001). The emerging role of the internal coach. *Consulting Psychology Journal: Practice and Research, 53* (4), 240–250.

Lee, R.J., & King, S.N. (2001). *Discovering the leader in you: A guide to realizing your personal leadership potential*. San Francisco, CA: Jossey-Bass.

McCall, M.W., Jr., Lombardo, M.M., & Morrison, A.M. (1988). *The lessons of experience: How successful executives develop on the job*. Lexington, MA: Lexington Books.

McCauley, C.D., Ruderman, M., Ohlott, P., & Morrow, J. (1994). Assessing the developmental components of managerial jobs. *Journal of Applied Psychology, 79* (4), 544–560.

Rosinski, P. (2003). *Coaching across cultures: New tools for leveraging national, corporate, and professional differences*. London: Nicholas Brealey.

Ethics

American Psychological Association. (2002). *Ethical principles of psychologists and code of conduct*. Washington, DC: Author.

Lowman, R.L. (1998). *The ethical practice of psychology in organizations*. Washington, DC: American Psychological Association.

How Coaching Is Done

Dotlich, D.L., & Cairo, P.C. (1999). *Action coaching*. San Francisco, CA: Jossey-Bass.

Dotlich, D.L., & Cairo, P.C. (2002). *Unnatural leadership: Going against intuition and experience to develop ten new leadership instincts*. San Francisco, CA: Jossey-Bass.

Flaherty, J. (1999). *Coaching: Evoking excellence in others*. Woburn, MA: Butterworth Heinemann.

Hargrove, R. (1995). *Masterful coaching*. San Francisco, CA: Pfeiffer.

Kilburg, R.R. (1996). Executive coaching [Special Issue]. *Consulting Psychology Journal: Practice and Research, 48* (2).

Kilburg, R.R. (2000). *Executive coaching: Developing managerial wisdom in a world of chaos*. Washington, DC: American Psychological Association.

O'Neill, M.B. (2000). *Executive coaching with backbone and heart*. San Francisco, CA: Jossey-Bass.

Whitmore, J. (1996). *Coaching for performance*. London: Nicholas Brealey.

Whitworth, L. (1998). *Co-active coaching*. Palo Alto, CA: Davies-Black.

Measuring and Managing Coaches

Corporate Leadership Council. (2003). *Maximizing returns on professional executive coaching*. Washington, DC: Corporate Executive Board.

Miller, K.K., & Hart, W. (2001). *Choosing an executive coach*. Greensboro, NC: Center for Creative Leadership.

Miller, K.K., & Hart, W. (2001). *Using your executive coach*. Greensboro, NC: Center for Creative Leadership.

Wasylyshyn, K.M. (2003). Executive coaching: An outcome study. *Consulting Psychology Journal: Practice and Research, 55* (2), 94–106.

Winum, P.C. (2003). Developing leadership: What is distinctive about what psychologists can offer? *Consulting Psychology Journal: Practice and Research, 55* (1), 41–46.

Witherspoon, R., & White, R.P. (1997). *Four essential ways that coaching can help executives*. Greensboro, NC: Center for Creative Leadership.

Overviews of Coaching

Douglas, C.A., & Morley, W.H. (2000). *Executive coaching: An annotated bibliography*. Greensboro, NC: Center for Creative Leadership.

Goldsmith, M., Lyons, L., & Freas, A. (2000). *Coaching for leadership: How the world's greatest coaches help leaders learn*. San Francisco, CA: Pfeiffer.

Hudson, F.M. (1999). *The handbook of coaching*. San Francisco, CA: Jossey-Bass.

Peterson, D.B. (2002). Management development: Coaching and mentoring programs. In K. Kraiger (Ed.), *Creating, implementing, and managing effective training and development*. San Francisco, CA: Jossey-Bass.

About the Authors

Anna Marie Valerio is president of Executive Leadership Strategies, LLC, a consulting firm specializing in executive coaching and the design and implementation of human resource and organization development solutions. Her areas of expertise include leadership development, organization and individual assessment, executive education strategy, and performance management.

Dr. Valerio's background includes consulting experience with Fortune 500 clients representing nearly every industrial sector. Prior to consulting, she held professional roles at IBM, Sony, and Verizon. She holds a Ph.D. in psychology from The City University of New York. Dr. Valerio is a member of the Society for Industrial-Organizational Psychology.

Robert J. Lee is a management consultant in private practice in New York City. He serves as a coach to executives regarding leadership and managerial effectiveness. From 1994 to 1997, he was president and CEO of the Center for Creative Leadership, the world's largest leadership development and research organization. For the prior twenty years, he was with Lee Hecht Harrison, an international career services and consulting firm, of which he was a founder.

Dr. Lee is on the adjunct faculty of the Milano Graduate School of New School University and Baruch College, CUNY, where he is also a senior fellow with the Zicklin Leadership Initiative. He teaches courses on executive coaching and is the director of the iCoachNewYork training program. He is on the faculty of the International Centre for the Study of Coaching, based at Middlesex University, London. His Ph.D., from Case Western Reserve University, is in I/O psychology. Dr. Lee is a member of the Society for Industrial-Organizational Psychology and of the NTL Institute.

Index

Pfeiffer Publications Guide

This guide is designed to familiarize you with the various types of Pfeiffer publications. The formats section describes the various types of products that we publish; the methodologies section describes the many different ways that content might be provided within a product. We also provide a list of the topic areas in which we publish.

FORMATS

In addition to its extensive book-publishing program, Pfeiffer offers content in an array of formats, from fieldbooks for the practitioner to complete, ready-to-use training packages that support group learning.

FIELDBOOK Designed to provide information and guidance to practitioners in the midst of action. Most fieldbooks are companions to another, sometimes earlier, work, from which its ideas are derived; the fieldbook makes practical what was theoretical in the original text. Fieldbooks can certainly be read from cover to cover. More likely, though, you'll find yourself bouncing around following a particular theme, or dipping in as the mood, and the situation, dictate.

HANDBOOK A contributed volume of work on a single topic, comprising an eclectic mix of ideas, case studies, and best practices sourced by practitioners and experts in the field.

An editor or team of editors usually is appointed to seek out contributors and to evaluate content for relevance to the topic. Think of a handbook not as a ready-to-eat meal, but as a cookbook of ingredients that enables you to create the most fitting experience for the occasion.

RESOURCE Materials designed to support group learning. They come in many forms: a complete, ready-to-use exercise (such as a game); a comprehensive resource on one topic (such as conflict management) containing a variety of methods and approaches; or a collection of like-minded activities (such as icebreakers) on multiple subjects and situations.

TRAINING PACKAGE An entire, ready-to-use learning program that focuses on a particular topic or skill. All packages comprise a guide for the facilitator/trainer and a workbook for the participants. Some packages are supported with additional media—such as video—or learning aids, instruments, or other devices to help participants understand concepts or practice and develop skills.

- *Facilitator/trainer's guide* Contains an introduction to the program, advice on how to organize and facilitate the learning event, and step-by-step instructor notes. The guide also contains copies of presentation materials—handouts, presentations, and overhead designs, for example—used in the program.

- *Participant's workbook* Contains exercises and reading materials that support the learning goal and serves as a valuable reference and support guide for participants in the weeks and months that follow the learning event. Typically, each participant will require his or her own workbook.

ELECTRONIC CD-ROMs and web-based products transform static Pfeiffer content into dynamic, interactive experiences. Designed to take advantage of the searchability, automation, and ease-of-use that technology provides, our e-products bring convenience and immediate accessibility to your workspace.

METHODOLOGIES

CASE STUDY A presentation, in narrative form, of an actual event that has occurred inside an organization. Case studies are not prescriptive, nor are they used to prove a point; they are designed to develop critical analysis and decision-making skills. A case study has a specific time frame, specifies a sequence of events, is narrative in structure, and contains a plot structure—an issue (what should be/have been done?). Use case studies when the goal is to enable participants to apply previously learned theories to the circumstances in the case, decide what is pertinent, identify the real issues, decide what should have been done, and develop a plan of action.

ENERGIZER A short activity that develops readiness for the next session or learning event. Energizers are most commonly used after a break or lunch to stimulate or refocus the group. Many involve some form of physical activity, so they are a useful way to counter post-lunch lethargy. Other uses include transitioning from one topic to another, where "mental" distancing is important.

EXPERIENTIAL LEARNING ACTIVITY (ELA) A facilitator-led intervention that moves participants through the learning cycle from experience to application (also known as a Structured Experience). ELAs are carefully thought-out designs in which there is a definite learning purpose and intended outcome. Each step—everything that participants do during the activity—facilitates the accomplishment of the stated goal. Each ELA includes complete instructions for facilitating the intervention and a clear statement of goals, suggested group size and timing, materials required, an explanation of the process, and, where appropriate, possible variations to the activity. (For more detail on Experiential Learning Activities, see the Introduction to the *Reference Guide to Handbooks and Annuals*, 1999 edition, Pfeiffer, San Francisco.)

GAME A group activity that has the purpose of fostering team spirit and togetherness in addition to the achievement of a pre-stated goal. Usually contrived—undertaking a desert expedition, for example—this type of learning method offers an engaging means for participants to demonstrate and practice business and interpersonal skills. Games are effective for team building and personal development mainly because the goal is subordinate to the process—the means through which participants reach decisions, collaborate, communicate, and generate trust and understanding. Games often engage teams in "friendly" competition.

ICEBREAKER A (usually) short activity designed to help participants overcome initial anxiety in a training session and/or to acquaint the participants with one another. An icebreaker can be a fun activity or can be tied to specific topics or training goals. While a useful tool in itself, the icebreaker comes into its own in situations where tension or resistance exists within a group.

INSTRUMENT A device used to assess, appraise, evaluate, describe, classify, and summarize various aspects of human behavior. The term used to describe an instrument depends primarily on its format and purpose. These terms include survey, questionnaire, inventory, diagnostic, survey, and poll. Some uses of instruments include providing instrumental feedback to group members, studying here-and-now processes or functioning within a group, manipulating group composition, and evaluating outcomes of training and other interventions.

Instruments are popular in the training and HR field because, in general, more growth can occur if an individual is provided with a method for focusing specifically on his or her own behavior. Instruments also are used to obtain information that will serve as a basis for change and to assist in workforce planning efforts.

Paper-and-pencil tests still dominate the instrument landscape with a typical package comprising a facilitator's guide, which offers advice on administering the instrument and interpreting the collected data, and an initial set of instruments. Additional instruments are available separately. Pfeiffer, though, is investing heavily in e-instruments. Electronic instrumentation provides effortless distribution and, for larger groups particularly, offers advantages over paper-and-pencil tests in the time it takes to analyze data and provide feedback.

LECTURETTE A short talk that provides an explanation of a principle, model, or process that is pertinent to the participants' current learning needs. A lecturette is intended to establish a common language bond between the trainer and the participants by providing a mutual frame of reference. Use a lecturette as an introduction to a group activity or event, as an interjection during an event, or as a handout.

MODEL A graphic depiction of a system or process and the relationship among its elements. Models provide a frame of reference and something more tangible, and more easily remembered, than a verbal explanation. They also give participants something to "go on," enabling them to track their own progress as they experience the dynamics, processes, and relationships being depicted in the model.

ROLE PLAY A technique in which people assume a role in a situation/scenario: a customer service rep in an angry-customer exchange, for example. The way in which the role is approached is then discussed and feedback is offered. The role play is often repeated using a different approach and/or incorporating changes made based on feedback received. In other words, role playing is a spontaneous interaction involving realistic behavior under artificial (and safe) conditions.

SIMULATION A methodology for understanding the interrelationships among components of a system or process. Simulations differ from games in that they test or use a model that depicts or mirrors some aspect of reality in form, if not necessarily in content. Learning occurs by studying the effects of change on one or more factors of the model. Simulations are commonly used to test hypotheses about what happens in a system—often referred to as "what if?" analysis—or to examine best-case/worst-case scenarios.

THEORY A presentation of an idea from a conjectural perspective. Theories are useful because they encourage us to examine behavior and phenomena through a different lens.

TOPICS

The twin goals of providing effective and practical solutions for workforce training and organization development and meeting the educational needs of training and human resource professionals shape Pfeiffer's publishing program. Core topics include the following:

Leadership & Management

Communication & Presentation

Coaching & Mentoring

Training & Development

E-Learning

Teams & Collaboration

OD & Strategic Planning

Human Resources

Consulting